SEEDTIME
and
HARVEST

CHRISTIE PURIFOY

HARVEST HOUSE PUBLISHERS
EUGENE, OREGON

While the earth remains, seedtime and harvest, cold and heat, summer and winter, day and night, shall not cease.

GENESIS 8:22 ESV

CONTENTS

Introduction: Everything Is Reconciled in a Garden 9

Part One: Gardens Grow Roots

The Ghost in My Garden 23

❊ Heirloom Roses for Dorothy 29

Gardens Visible and Invisible 31

How to Change the World in Three Easy Steps 37

❊ Special Shade Plants to Inspire the Planting of Trees 43

Roots and Wind 45

❊ Favorite Ornamental Grasses 52

The Spirit of a Place 55

❊ How to Make New Plants in Water 61

Part Two: Gardens Grow Connection

A Harvest for the Birds 65

Creepy, Crawly Wonders 71

❊ Butterfly and Plant Pairs 77

Raining Dogs and Cats and Chickens 79

❊ Chickens in the Garden 85

Making Friends with the Neighbors 87

❊ Ornamental Food 93

Sharing the Garden 95

❊ Plants the Deer Do Not Care to Share 101

Part Three: Gardens Grow Wholeness

A Hodgepodge and a Mishmash 105

   ❋ A Tea Garden 111

Native Plants and Kindness 113

   ❋ Seedheads to Savor 119

Controlling the Uncontrollable Vine 121

   ❋ Well-Behaved Vines and Climbers 127

A Layered Garden 131

   ❋ Ground-Huggers 139

Whole Gardens for Whole Gardeners 143

Part Four: Gardens Grow Hope

The Art of Wildness 151

   ❋ Fully Alive Lawns 157

The Generous Garden 159

   ❋ Planting for the Future 164

Choose Your Own Adventure 167

   ❋ Ground Cherry Jam 174

Hope Is Brown Then Green 177

   ❋ A Year in Bulbs 183

Hope Is Green Then Red 185

Epilogue: Hope in an Age of Climate Chaos 191

INTRODUCTION

Everything Is Reconciled in a Garden

Between the first deep freeze of fall and the last deep freeze of spring, while the ground beneath my feet cycles between stone hard and mud melt, I walk the same route through my neighborhood nearly every day. During the growing season, I am too busy tending my garden to walk. Occasionally, I wander the same path late on a summer evening, but only when I am frustrated with my garden and looking for escape. It is January in Pennsylvania as I write these words. I walked my familiar winter route today, a path that carries me over sidewalks, along a public golf course, and behind many of the houses built ten years ago on the farmland that originally gave my old farmhouse its purpose. Behind one of these houses, I am always cheered to see a small raised-bed garden. Because I mostly walk this way in winter, I have never been sure if the garden is still cultivated. Today, it was covered in dead plant material—weeds or vegetables, I could not say—along with a few rusty tomato cages. Somehow the sight of it always pleases me more than the neat but sterile landscapes of the homes nearby. These

Gardening teaches us that we belong to nature and are also responsible for it. Human culture and nature's destiny are inextricably intertwined.

VIGEN GUROIAN, *INHERITING PARADISE*

tumble-down raised beds tell me that someone has been involved with this place beyond the minimum we expect of a homeowner. Someone wanted more than lawn grass and shrubs.

A longing for Eden—for paradise—is buried deep in every human heart. Some are more aware of *paradise lost* than others. For these, the weedy and overgrown vegetable beds in a corner of the backyard are not the sign of failure they first appear to be. Rather, they suggest that someone has listened to her heart. Someone has sought a good and right connection with the natural world. Others may be less aware that anything of importance is missing from their lives. Convinced they were born with black thumbs, they ignore the houseplants for sale at the supermarket. They pursue only those hobbies far removed from green, growing life. They are content with a landscape that fulfills the minimum requirements of their homeowners' association bylaws. However, gardening is something much more than home maintenance. Gardening is no mere hobby. It is not a pastime intended only to help us "pass the time." Gardening is a way of life, and as a way of life, it can cure so much that ails us.

After all, our world is on intimate terms with estrangement. We can each tell stories of fractured friendships, neighborly disputes, even nations at war. Endangered species lists, "save the Amazon" campaigns, and even that new parking lot where a meadow once grew remind us of the enmity that seems to taint our human relationships with the natural world. If we have dared to plant a seed or pull a weed, we can tell tales of droughts and heat waves and failure. But with so much around us out of tune, we gardeners also testify to regular wonders. Our cups runneth over with zinnias and zucchini every July. We are maybe just a little bit tired of sweet, sun-warmed tomatoes by September. It is true that when we garden, we are *more* aware of the broken things. Tomatoes are meant to turn a glorious red, but sometimes high heat keeps them stubbornly green. Drought is often par for the course in August, but surely not in May?

Yet despite the crack that does indeed seem to run through everything, we see firsthand in the garden how winter gives way to spring, decay feeds the green of new life, and every last seed, insect, butterfly, and bird is connected. To one another. And to us.

When sounds are unreconciled and disconnected, the result is cacophony and noise. When sounds are put in right relationship to one another, the result is music. In a world out of tune, gardeners cultivate harmony. The wonder is that there are almost infinite possibilities for harmony, whether we are speaking about the art of music or the art of gardening. There is no single way to reconcile soil with seed with sunlight. When we set out to cultivate the music of life, the song is always new, always changing, always surprising, always good. Life cannot be static, or it ceases to be life. Life is growth. And what are we growing in a garden? Whether the tangible fruit is a tomato or a rosebud, in a garden, we are growing roots. We are growing connection. We are growing wholeness. And we are growing hope.

I sometimes think I was born rootless. While others around me seemed to thrive in the heat and humidity and cowboy culture of central Texas, I usually felt like an observer rather than a participant (though an orchard of pecan trees will always make my heart sing). Today I suspect that my sensitive temperament only made me aware at a young age of something that is true for each one of us: we are never born with roots—we grow them. It may be that we receive the work of previous generations. Perhaps our great-grandparents and grandparents and parents cultivated places and cultures within which we can, in time, feel as rooted as they. But perhaps not. Perhaps like me, you leave the home of your birth, either by choice or by necessity, and must figure out how to belong and where. At its core, gardening is not about the roses or dahlias or tomatoes we might grow. At its core, gardening is an intimate, ongoing relationship with a place. And it is this relationship that roots us as firmly as a tree is rooted in the ground.

We have always understood trees as rooted, but we have mistaken them as solitary in their rootedness. In recent years, scientists have discovered that a forest is less like a collection of individual trees and more like a single organism connected underground by its roots. Even sick or injured or dying trees with no leaves for photosynthesis can be kept alive through the roots they share with other trees. A tree that is fully and completely rooted is also a tree that is fully connected. Rootedness and connectedness are one and the same. I began to garden because I like to eat good food, and I wanted flavors that could not be found in supermarkets. But my pursuit of good food led me, eventually, to flowers. And through the flowers, I began to feel connected to the pollinators who feasted on them, the butterflies who danced on them, and the birds who couldn't seem to stay away. My relationship with a particular place has become a connection to the various and abundant life of this place—and life is so much more than a few fresh flavors on our dinner plate.

The buzz and hum of garden life can be noisy in a way. I am never not startled by the chattering and quarreling of squirrels in the old walnut tree that towers over our black-painted barn. And every year I forget how loud our chickens are at sunrise until that first autumn cool front arrives, and I once again sleep with the window beside my bed left open. When I write of the music of the garden, I do not mean that its sounds never grate on my ear. Rather, these sounds—whether from my dog barking at the neighbor's dog or from the children who live next door shouting and squealing while they pick the wild wineberries that grow along our fence line—somehow add up to a wholeness that is pulsing with life. This is not the peace of "peace and quiet." This is the peace of *shalom*, that ancient Hebrew word that means peace, harmony, and *wholeness*. We are fragmented people in a fragmented world, but we do not feel made for fragmentation. No matter the form of our religion, no matter the shape of our spiritual lives, we long for a mode of being and

relating in which the puzzle pieces fit, in which the picture—whatever exactly it depicts—is beautiful.

I have often shocked my garden visitors by declaring that my garden is not my happy place. Though my intention in this book is to recruit more of you to the ranks of gardeners, I make that task harder by admitting that my garden often feels like a battleground. It isn't so much that I do battle with pests and weeds. I am learning more and more to fight that fight through surrender. I cover my soil instead of disrupting it, because every tug is a signal to some weed seed to wake up. I no longer do direct battle with pests; instead, I choose to grow different plants or I try to entice natural predators. It is a sly, sideways form of war. The true battle being waged in my garden is internal, inside of *me*. It is the battle I wage because of what gardening calls out within me: anxiety and peace, fear and hope, wonder and despair. I am tugged between my longing for beauty and the reality of a disease-ridden flower. I am filled with joy by the freshness of spring only to feel it wither in the oppressive heat of summer. In the garden, all my internal monsters are awakened, and I must learn how to defeat them or soothe them or transform them. If I spend one hour pulling weeds, often I emerge more changed than my garden.

Both garden and gardener are constantly shifting. In a garden, after all, nothing stays the same, not even for a day. At first glance, the inexorable patterns of nature might seem oppressive. Thousands of years ago, a wise one wrote that "the sun rises and the sun sets. . . . What has been will be again, what has been done will be done again; there is nothing new under the sun" (Ecclesiastes 1:5, 9). If there is indeed nothing new under the sun, then the pressure is off, isn't it? If our life is really only "breath," as the same writer claims, then let us drop our inflated sense of importance—that view of ourselves that says we must conquer the world and change the world—and get down to the humble business of quietly tending the bit of the world that lies right at our fingertips. Yes, the world is in need of changing. Enmity and brokenness are all around. But in a garden, enemies are reconciled, our own turbulent hearts find peace, and the final fruit of our efforts is a stubborn and persistent hope.

Our human inheritance is an eagerness to climb stairways to heaven and send rockets to the moon. We dream big and aim high, yet ironically it is when we bend low to the ground, when we give our full attention to the dirt right around our feet, when we devote ourselves to tending and caring and planting, that we really do change the world. Gardens grow much more than plants: gardens grow *life*. Gardens grow thriving connections among fungi and insects, birds and animals, people and neighborhoods. When we care for a garden, we are caring for our own selves, and we are caring for the entire green and blue jewel that is the garden of planet Earth. Your pots of herbs on the windowsill may seem isolated and small, but they are a link with your neighbor's tomato bed, which is a link with the community garden, and a link to the forest preserve, the botanical garden, the organic farm—all of them joining up to wind the earth round in green ribbons of life. From seedtime to harvest and back again, the reconciling work of a garden is never finished, always ongoing, and, in every season, eager for us to join in and receive the *more* that is our heart's desire.

PART ONE

GARDENS GROW ROOTS

*It's the time you spent on your rose that makes
your rose so important. . . People have forgotten
this truth. . . But you mustn't forget it. You become
responsible forever for what you've tamed.
You're responsible for your rose.*

ANTOINE DE SAINT-EXUPÉRY, *THE LITTLE PRINCE*

THE GHOST
IN MY GARDEN

Sometimes ghosts announce themselves by ringing your doorbell. Four days ago, I was sorting laundry into piles on my bedroom floor while two men used chainsaws to attack the enormous girth of an old Norway maple only a few yards from my front door. The men were familiar friends by now. We've hired the same tree removal company repeatedly over the past ten years as our old maples have—one by one and sometimes two or three at a time—succumbed to age. Up on the second floor of this redbrick farmhouse, I could feel the entire building tremble whenever another section of the old tree fell to the ground, as if a giant stone had dropped into a giant pond and the waves were washing right over me and my house. That is when the doorbell rang. Between the barking of our dog and the whine of the saws, it is understandable if I thought the small group gathered on my porch were neighbors come to complain about the noise.

I assumed I was about to be shamed or taken to task. I thought I would need to defend our decision to bring in the chainsaws. So when the bearded man in front of me said, "I used to climb that tree," I countered, "It was hollow. All the way down it was hollow."

Then he told me his name—or shouted it, rather—and the name rang a bell even louder than the dog, louder than the saws, and I said, "That's my name too!" I remembered then how ten years ago my husband and I had stepped past the

For Sale sign and through this door and been handed papers listing all the families who had ever called this place—Maplehurst—*home*. Fifty years before, a family with my maiden name had lived here with their many children. I had received this as a sign, and we moved in three weeks later. Now here was a little boy from that long-ago family. He was all grown up, newly retired from work that had taken him far from Pennsylvania, and, once invited in, bursting with boyish eagerness to show his wife and adult daughters the family place, to tell his stories of climbing trees and falling down stairs and watching his mother make wineberry jam in the kitchen.

He told me her name—his mother—and in that moment I finally had a name for the ghost in my garden. "She loved flowers," he said. "She gave tours at Longwood Gardens just down the road," he said. "She tended azaleas, and she grew roses. Especially," he said, "she grew roses." Here, then, in the flesh and blood of his stories, I had the name of the ghostly gardener whose path I had

so often traced through the brambles that edged our property. I had glimpsed her shadow in the azalea shrubs that still bloom each spring in bright colors beneath the old hemlock and pine. I had spotted her touch in the hostas that emerge each summer deep in a bramble patch that must once have been a neat garden bed. I had thought hostas a more contemporary garden plant, but a little research told me that the very first American hosta society had organized itself in the 1960s in Swarthmore, Pennsylvania, not so very far away from Maplehurst.

I encountered my garden ghost most directly on a day in late spring while weeding my daylily patch on the earthen bank that once gave hay wagons access to the second-floor hayloft of a Pennsylvania-style bank barn. The breeze had picked up, and I suddenly smelled perfume: *rose* perfume. My daylilies were only a half-hearted attempt to reclaim this side of the old bank from the brambles and weed trees and invasive multiflora roses that are a pervasive nuisance in my part of Pennsylvania. But multiflora roses do not smell like a spilled bottle of perfume. Curious, I hunted out the source of the smell and found a bubble-gum pink rose, half hidden by weeds but nevertheless climbing the ruined stone foundation of the barn. This was no thorny multiflora. This was a gardener's rose, and now I knew who planted it. Her name was Dorothy.

I walked Dorothy's family through the entire house, apologizing for the laundry piles, the state of the teenager's bedroom, the stack of cardboard I had intended to carry down to the basement recycling bin. Dorothy's son asked if any of his mother's roses remained. I looked away and said only, "No," unable to admit that the pretty rose I discovered by its scent had been lost again when the landscape crew hired by the surrounding neighborhood overzealously sprayed and mowed their side of the old barn bank. "Her azaleas are still here," I told him, "and I am planting roses. If you come back this summer, I will show you the roses." Then he lifted the dog crate from beneath my son's bedroom window and, with a huge grin on his face, showed me the black marks on the wood floor. His brother, he explained, had once lit the curtains on fire playing with candles.

When my husband came home later that same day, he asked if our visitor had been sad, if he had been grieved to see how much had changed. But I knew he had not been sad. Not at all. He had been delighted. It was with delight that he told me he once climbed the tree chainsaws were erasing and with delight that he handed me a dozen other stories like a memory bouquet from the past. Even those black spots on the floor had delighted him. It didn't seem to matter that the roses were gone or that the huge tree was shaking us with its going. If anything, our piles and messes and noise seemed to prove the house that had held so much living was still here. Still full. Still alive. A son still slept in the burn-marked room. A mother still grew roses in the garden.

I had always planted into an absence—names I did not know, stories I'd never heard, and only a few lingering plants and trees to prove that someone else had once cared. But the blank page of the past was suddenly teeming with life: little boys tumbling down stairs, sticky-sweet steam rising from a jampot, and the branches of a copper beech tree tapping a bedroom window in invitation, like a living ladder begging some boy to escape on midnight adventures. But on the final day of a giant tree's life, I realized that all the losses and hard changes meant that this place was alive and growing and had never stopped growing. Nothing—not a tree, not a person, not a place—grows without changing, and where there is no growth, there is no life. From seedtime to harvest and back again, this place remains. Our earth remains. I am sinking my roots down deep with every pile of laundry and every tray of seedlings and every tree trimmed or cut down or planted. This is not the end. This is the beginning.

HEIRLOOM ROSES FOR DOROTHY

I have grown every one of these heirloom beauties here at Maplehurst. Now I tend them in memory of Dorothy and in hope for those gardeners who will one day follow me.

'Ballerina' (1937)
This rose is as sweet and dainty as its name suggests. I planted three of them on top of the old barn bank because the flowers remind me of Dorothy's rose that was found and lost again. 'Ballerina' has open-faced flowers with a simple ring of pink and white petals around bright yellow stamens.

'Cecile Brunner' (1881)
Nicknamed the "Sweetheart Rose," this is a cultivar whose flowers were once favored because they made the ideal boutonniere. I planted the climbing variety to cascade over our tall wire chicken run.

'The Fairy' (1932)
One of the first roses I ever planted at Maplehurst, this sweet, small, pink rose is a healthy super-bloomer in summer.

'Albertine' (1921)
The ruffled, apricot-colored flowers of this climbing rose only bloom once in spring, but what a bloom it is. Once-blooming heirlooms are ideal in my garden because the flowers finish well before the destructive Japanese beetles come out.

'American Beauty' (1909)
This may be the most fragrant climbing rose I have ever grown. Large, dark pink, cupped flowers only bloom once, but they bloom in profusion for days, even weeks. This is a floral encounter to anticipate all year long.

GARDENS VISIBLE
AND INVISIBLE

I have lived in my current home, this farmhouse called Maplehurst, for only ten years, but so much of what I have planted has already vanished. I planted spruce trees the deer ate. I planted rhododendrons the heavy clay soil suffocated. I planted an entire vegetable garden with a dozen raised beds and a white picket fence, and I cultivated it intensely for five years before we demolished it to reroute our driveway. I planted a patch of asparagus that later became a cut flower garden. I planted a slope with daylilies that were eventually overcome by brambles and weeds. I planted three crab apples in a too-shady spot, and they slowly declined unto death over just a few years. If you were to tell me this all sounds like monumental failure, I would respond by asking you, "What are we really growing in our gardens? Plants? Or roots?" Because while so many individual plants have vanished, my own roots are now sunk deep in the earth of this hilltop home.

My relationship with this place, this redbrick house embedded in Pennsylvania clay soil, is not defined by my failures. Rather, it is defined by my effort. I have dreamed here and sweated here and dug up the ground here. Many of the changes I have effected are still visible. There are the climbing roses that billow over the split-rail fence near the shade garden. There are the three white-flowering dogwood trees in the driveway's central circular planting bed, the ones that look like sparkling jets of water when they bloom in spring. There is the young saucer

magnolia tree we planted to mirror the enormous old saucer magnolia on the other side of the driveway. It was so small when we first planted it that it flowered almost invisibly for three springs before suddenly, one recent April day, it began to look exactly like the thing we had intended it to be: a youthful reflection of the venerable tree across from it and my gift to future generations. The old tree my daughters often danced beneath in blizzards of pink, perfumed petals will not live forever. But years from now, someone else's daughter will twirl under the tree I planted.

My efforts have established other lasting changes that are not visible. This place has made me its expert. I know where the frost pools in the low places, where the deer tend to walk, where the groundhog always digs a new tunnel door. I know from which direction the winter wind blows and where rainbows always appear in the summer sky. I know how bright the shade is beneath the magnolia in spring and how deep and dark that shade becomes in July. I am the world's only living expert on this place, and I am rooted here, I am at home here, because I know and am known only here. I do not garden because any particular garden, or any particular plant, must live forever. That is not the proper scale for judging this work. The enormous vegetable garden I tended in the spot where we now park our cars is still alive in me. Everything I learned there, every variety I tried there, every effort that failed there, I will carry all of that intimate knowledge to the new vegetable garden I am planning in the southwestern corner of our back garden. The new vegetable garden will also have raised beds, but instead of mulch between the beds—so heavy to spread! so prone to growing weeds!—I will leave the sod. I think I will be grateful for those cool green paths when I am digging up fingerling potatoes on a hot day in July.

I can already hear the protestations. "You own your home! You intend to stay! But I am a renter. I am transient. I have no idea where I will live next spring." But here is the wild truth about human roots: we grow them and go on growing them even while we wander. It matters much less *where* we live; what matters most is *how* we live in each place. Our own roots are one of the invisible fruits of the visible garden. My roots began to grow when I was but a child in my father's Texas garden. Though I generally retreated indoors during the hot days of summer, his garden was a paradise in spring. Because of my father's garden, I have always known that with time and effort, even inhospitable ground could be made to flower. Years later, these latent roots were stirred by the springtime beauty of my new home in northern Virginia. I had never witnessed that sharp dividing line between winter and spring that exists in northern climates. One day there is only brown death. The very next, it seems, the woods are laced with purple redbuds. Much later, in a community garden on the South Side of Chicago, my roots really began to reach and sink. I grieved the loss of that garden when the construction vehicles rolled in, but the roots I grew there prepared me to make a home and a garden at Maplehurst in Pennsylvania. Nothing is ever wasted. Even our dead plants feed the soil.

A rooted life is not a life in which we never move, never say goodbye, never begin again. Change is inevitable, even for a deeply rooted tree. But a rooted life is opposed to the superficial life, in which we are always skating over surfaces, our way smoothed by a ubiquitous consumerism. In a superficial life, place does not matter. We drink the same coffee shop drink, we drive the same asphalt roads, we spend our leisure time in the same chain stores, chain restaurants, enjoy the same chain experiences. Such a life can feel inevitable for many of us, and I am not immune to its easy, comfortable appeal. But it does not take much to crack open the perfect bubble of a superficial life. Only attempt to grow a container of herbs or flowers by the back door, and you will begin to watch for rain, you will fear the wind that knocks your container over, you will notice the angle of the sun as you adjust your plant for more light, you will observe the smallest bee who comes to visit, and suddenly it matters that you are exactly where you are. And—before you even know it—you are rooted.

HOW TO CHANGE
THE WORLD IN THREE
EASY STEPS

Step one: choose a tree. Admittedly, this is the most difficult step and will likely take the longest. But take your time! Our choice of a tree to plant can alter a place for generations. There is no need to hurry this decision. Step two: dig a hole. It is perfectly acceptable to hire out this portion of the task. I recommend asking around for a nine-year-old boy. In my experience, they love to dig holes and ask only to be paid in candy. Step three: plant your tree and water it well. Admittedly, even a very tall sapling, of the sort that is sold in a large container, will not at first appear to change the world very much. In fact, your skinny baby tree, in the beginning, might be difficult even to see. You might choose to circle it with wire mesh to protect it from hungry deer or lawn mowers, from rambunctious dogs or children. But small trees settle in quickly, and in only a handful of years you will have created that precious, cooling global commodity: shade.

Trees make places. Where once was nothing, merely open space like a kind of erasure on a map, with the planting of a tree it becomes an entire world unto itself. To bow beneath the canopy of a leafy tree is to enter a secret, hidden place where heat and sunlight are tempered and—depending on the variety of tree—a thousand kinds of living beings might make their home. Oak trees, for instance, support more life forms than any other North American tree, providing food and shelter for countless insects, spiders, birds, and mammals. An oak tree, especially if the leaf litter is left to lie where it falls, is like a thriving metropolis of life. It is a whole ecosystem unto itself and can turn a typical suburban deadscape of fertilized and irrigated lawn grass into a thriving, flourishing lifescape. Delaware entomologist Doug Tallamy is on a mission to encourage as many of us as possible to plant our gardens with native oaks. His oak tree advocacy began with the study of caterpillars, a life form so small that most of us stop noticing them once we leave childhood. But caterpillars are the foundation of the earth's food system, and oak trees support more caterpillar species than any other North American plant.

If a gardener makes it her goal to grow life, then an oak tree is the easiest and most direct route to success. If a gardener has made it her goal to grow sunflowers or roses, then an oak tree might seem like a mistake. The late gardening columnist for the *Washington Post*, Henry Mitchell, with his famous tongue-in-cheek wit, wrote that he expected "all my other sins to be forgiven in reward for one proud virtue: I have never in my life planted a tree in the smack dab middle of the garden where it would prevent the growth of virtually all desirable flowers."[1] He then goes on to describe the glory of tree after tree so that a reader might be forgiven for wondering why a choice spot for a tree should be sacrificed merely for a rosebush.

It was the memory of my father's own beautiful rose garden that drew me to gardening as an adult. The magnetic pull of an exquisite, scented rose is strong, but after ten years of growing roses I discovered the quiet splendor of shade gardening. Flower power is often more subtle in the shade, and most of it is displayed in spring before the trees fully leaf out. However, the same gardening chores like planting and weeding that are torture in the full sunshine of a hot summer day become pleasant and refreshing in a shade garden. Roses are wonderful, but the

cool greenness of yew layered on ferns layered on hostas can be enjoyed without feeling the burn of sweat and sunscreen running into my eyes. In the shade, gardening becomes fun again. And for those who might be saying, "What about peonies?" I have good news. The woodland peonies from Asia prefer shade. Indeed, their delicate single flowers and jewellike seedpods fairly shine in the dappled light beneath a tall tree.

Trees are placemakers. They shape and then tell the story of a place like few other plants can. What would Savannah, Georgia, be without live oaks dripping in Spanish moss? What would my own Chester County, Pennsylvania, be without the majestic white oaks called Penn Oaks because they were already growing when William Penn last visited his fledgling colony? Tropical islands have their palm trees, mountaintops their fir forests, and even the desert southwest its treelike saguaro. Trees are living, rooted sculptures, and they entirely alter our experience of a place. In this way, they give us not only shade but a quality that is recognizable and inspires our affection and attachment. Trees are the face of a place, and like the face of our beloved, they tell us clearly, "Here is your home."

SPECIAL SHADE PLANTS TO INSPIRE THE PLANTING OF TREES

1. **Corydalis:** Relatives to the bleeding hearts, many corydalis varieties possess flowers that rise elegantly above ferny foliage.

2. **Hellebore** (*Helleborus* species and varieties): Not only are hellebores low growing, perennial, and happy in shade, but while it is still winter, they flower in rich colors from white and pink through burgundy and black.

3. **Windflowers** or Japanese anemone (*Anemone hupehensis* var. *japonica* and *Anemone* × *hybrida*): These beautiful open-faced flowers float on tall stems and dance in every breeze in late summer and early fall; my favorite variety is 'Honorine Jobert'.

4. **Siberian bugloss** or perennial forget-me-not (*Brunnera macrophylla*): Less aggressive than forget-me-nots, this perennial has fuzzy, heart-shaped leaves and delicate blue flowers in spring; I love the variety 'Jack Frost' for its splashes of silver.

5. **Toad lilies** (*Tricyrtis*): These shade-loving plants bloom in late summer and early fall. The delicate, spotted flowers always invite a closer look.

ROOTS AND WIND

W hen I was a child, I was more afraid of pampas grass than anything that might snatch at my ankles from underneath the bed. Pampas grass was a popular landscape plant in the 1970s. Given that it can live a decade or more, my 1980s childhood was littered with enormous specimens like shaggy monsters. Our neighbors had two gigantic stands of the grass flanking the entrance to their driveway. One summer, they invited us to swim in their backyard pool as often as we liked, but my father warned us about those grasses. "They look soft," he said, "but they can cut like razors." Even more frightening was my father's suggestion that the grass blades were particularly dangerous if swallowed. I thought of the sword swallowers I had seen in cartoons and picture books and should have felt safe—why would I ever place a blade of pampas grass inside my mouth?—but my father's words somehow evoked for me a grass blade that *wanted* to hurt me. We swam all summer, but before and after each visit, I squeezed past those grasses by walking in the exact center of the driveway, making myself small with arms wrapped tight around my middle.

Perhaps it was this early nightmare about an ornamental grass that accounts for my long delay in adding ornamental grasses to my garden at Maplehurst. Or perhaps it is only because I grew up on the prairie grasslands of central Texas where grasses bleached white with winter cold or summer drought were only—so I thought—the slightly dull backdrop to blue wildflowers or prickly cactus. Grass simply existed. Weren't ornamental gardens meant for colorful flowers that would never grow without a gardener's intervention? Wasn't grass the plant that romped wild in the place only *before* you planted a garden? I couldn't imagine giving space to a grass that might otherwise be given to a peony, no matter how "ornamental."

The first crack in my determined dislike of garden grasses came when Lurie Garden opened in Chicago during the decade we lived in that city. It moved me in a way that no garden really had previously. It wasn't only pretty—it was powerful, as if a wild prairie had been condensed and compressed into its most beautiful form and then unleashed within the city. A few years later, I walked the High Line in New York City and fell in love with the contrast of solid, unmoving buildings against delicate grass blades, seedheads, and peeling tree bark. Both of these urban gardens were designed by Dutch garden designer Piet Oudolf. The High Line transformed a disused elevated train track into a prairie path winding its way above the Hudson riverfront. The plant life I had taken for granted in Texas was just the thing to introduce a bit of softened nature into some of the hardest places. And after ten years of city life and having begun to make a garden at a farmhouse surrounded by suburbia rather than farmland, I craved the natural appearance of meadows and prairies and other semi-wild landscapes.

That word *landscape* evokes museum walls filled with framed images of mountains and fields. In other words, it evokes two-dimensional pictures. And when I first began to garden, I approached the task like a painter. I thought of flowers as decorative touches to a scene, as if I were adding daubs of pink and apricot to a backdrop of green. I should have realized my error much sooner. Raised amidst Texas prairie grasses in a family whose members occasionally picked up oil paints, I had lived in close proximity to many paintings of faded barns, barbed wire fences, and prairie grasses. How could I have not realized that the single biggest difference between a painting of grass and the real thing outside was movement? How could I have forgotten that grass responds to wind like almost nothing else in a garden?

Finally determined to add some movement to my garden—and with it a sense of aliveness—I tiptoed into the world of ornamental grasses with colorful and easy-to-love pink muhly grass and purple fountain grass. Neither is perennial in my garden (though the muhly grass should be if planted into some dry, fast-draining bed in spring and allowed to grow its roots well all summer), but purple fountain grass in particular became a fast favorite for containers. The fluffy purple florets that emerged in late summer were especially beautiful in flower arrangements with soft pink and apricot flowers, like dahlia and rose. However, neither of these candy-colored grasses would give my garden that naturalistic Oudolf effect. So I turned to a grass that Oudolf himself has used in many of his designs: prairie dropseed. One spring, I planted an experimental row of prairie dropseed plugs, mail-ordered from an online native plant nursery, in the sunny front edge of my home's foundation bed. By summer's end, the plug plants had spread into soft tussocks and were sending up tall, delicate spikelets of flower that smelled toasty, almost like popcorn. Backlit in the morning by the rising sun and—from another angle—backlit by the setting sun in evening, the flowers glowed like spun gold. When the breeze moved, the flowers responded and the whole garden seemed somehow more awake. "Success!" I thought, and promptly ordered a few hundred plugs for the next year's planting.

Like so many garden plants, my prairie dropseed grasses have performed well in some spots (generally, the sunnier and dryer places) and less well in others (I fear the beds underneath my white-flowering crepe myrtle trees really are too shady for them). But my experiment with prairie dropseed led to other experiments. 'Hameln' and 'Praline,' dwarf forms of fountain grass, are new favorites. The flowering spikelets aren't as delicate as the dropseed (they are more like the plumes on a purple fountain grass), but the way they catch the light is also incredible. I have seen 'Praline' glow like a torch. For shadier spots, *Chasmanthium latifolium*, often called river oats or northern sea oats, is a lush green option, though it sets seed and spreads itself around vigorously. But the way those seedheads turn ruddy bronze in fall and the way they rustle percussively in the wind makes me love their aggressive wildness.

I think decorator gardens, like decorator cakes piped with rosettes and curlicues of flowers, are just right for some gardeners and some places. But Maplehurst and I have wanted something more deeply rooted in natural, untouched places. We wanted grass seeds that danced and fed birds and spread as they once did unimpeded on this North American continent. Some grasses are invasive and do not belong in particular ecosystems, but others, if we choose wisely and well, help blur the line between cultivated and wild. And this is much more than an aesthetic preference. This is not simply about garden style. This is something many of us need—living always surrounded by too much asphalt—in order to feel rooted in our homes.

FAVORITE ORNAMENTAL GRASSES

Here I dive in where angels fear to tread. It is a slightly dangerous thing to recommend an ornamental grass. That pampas grass lesson runs deep in me, as it should, and I am aware that the Mexican feathergrass (Nassella tenuissima) I love in a container is an aggressive and alien spreader in the warmer, dryer climates. Please do your own research to determine whether these grasses will play nicely in your own garden. Keep in mind that just because a plant is offered for sale at a local nursery is no guarantee it is a good choice ecologically.

1. **'Karl Foerster' feather reed grass** (*Calamagrostis acutiflora* 'Karl Foerster'): Though it's not native to North America, I love this non-spreading grass as a vertical exclamation point in the garden. The spikelets look especially good once they are bleached blond in later summer.

2. **Purple fountain grass** (*Pennisetum setaceum* 'Rubrum'): Because it's not hardy below 20 degrees Fahrenheit, I grow this grass as an annual for its beautiful dark purple foliage and burgundy foxtail-like plumes. It looks wonderful in arrangements with pale pink and apricot flowers.

3. **'Hameln' dwarf fountain grass** (*Pennisetum alopecuroides* 'Hameln'): 'Hameln' is a beautiful, small perennial fountain grass that doesn't grow beyond three feet high or wide. It can take a little shade, and the birds in my garden love it.

4. **Japanese forest grass** (*Hakonechloa macra*): This is a beautiful and not-too-large perennial grass for shade. The green (or gold, if you choose a variety like 'All Gold') foliage falls in tidy, fountain-like waves.

5. **Prairie dropseed** (*Sporobolus heterolepis*): This is an elegant North American native prairie grass. It is a heat-loving, clumping (not spreading) grass that can seed itself around a bit, though it is not an aggressive self-sower in my own garden. In late summer, dropseed sends up airy panicles of flower on delicate stems. These seedheads persist in cold weather (though they are too delicate to stay upright beneath snow). Those with rich soil or heavy clay might substitute **fox sedge** (*Carex vulpinoidea*) for a similar look.

THE SPIRIT
OF A PLACE

During my childhood, my Texas hometown received brief notoriety when it was named by some now-forgotten media institution as one of the very "best." Was it best small town? Best for quality of life? Best for raising a family? I can no longer remember, but I do remember how a big-city reporter visited our "best of" town only to write a scathing rebuttal to the ranking. How could our place be "best" when our downtown business district was so small? So derelict? How could we be "best" when the only shopping mall was over the city line in the town right next door? How could such a dull, brown place be good, let alone "best"?

The reporter's inability to see the good in our place was a scandal to us and to our neighbors. I can remember how our family took the reporter's criticisms and argued them down, one by one, as we sat around our dinner table. "Oh, if only that reporter had knocked on our door! We could have told him why our home really was the best!" I laugh remembering how our egos had been hurt, because I also remember how my father bemoaned our town's excessive heat and humidity after every summer vacation spent in the Colorado Rockies. I remember how my mother would complain about the post oak trees that were just about the only trees in our area. Why so many post oaks when the live oaks in other Texas towns were so much prettier? And I remember how my parents would pile all four of us kids into the family station wagon for regular trips to the big city of Houston to find wonders we could not access in our small town: things like a big shopping mall with an ice-skating rink and an international food market that sold the Greek olives my mother loved and the sticky rice my father wanted. In truth, the only good thing we generally said about our place, at least amongst ourselves, was that it was home.

My father was a gardener, and in between complaints about the excessive summer heat and the salty soil, he was diligently cultivating something much more important than a garden: he was growing a relationship with our place. In the North Texas farming family in which he had been raised, an intimate relationship with the land was a given. Without it they would have gone hungry. Without it there would have been no money for new shoes, new overalls, or the rough paper tablets and fat crayons required by the local schoolteacher. There would have been no necktie or best dress for Sunday-morning church. Today, for most of us, a relationship with the ground beneath our feet feels optional. It is something we can pursue, like a hobby, or ignore in favor of travel or in deference to a long commute. But not for my father when he was a child. And not for my father when he was an adult. The farm had taught him well, and he could not—he would not—leave our brown backyard to its own devices. He would transform it into our Texas Eden, and it would feed us mulberries and blackberries and plums. It would give us cobbler and jam and bouquets of heirloom roses.

I imagine that long-ago ranking of our town's merits weighed data like unemployment rates and median income and access to hospital care. Maybe it also counted days of sunshine or the availability of green space. Such things matter, but they tell us little about the spirit of a place. I think we were so offended by the journalist's criticisms because we knew that our experience of our place could not be summed up with economic bullet points. Every place—if it hasn't been completely obliterated by asphalt and chain stores—has its own unique spirit.

The spirit of my hometown could be found in the ubiquitous post oak trees and their bounty of acorns, in the bluebonnet wildflowers flowing alongside the highway like water each spring, and in the university traditions that united us. It could be found in the public park where children fed ducks, in the churches where we gathered with neighbors on Sundays, in the public neighborhood pools where we cooled off on hot summer days.

I'm not sure it's possible to grow roots in completely anonymous places. The spirit of a place—even if that spirit is not always pleasant—is the part of the place we are able to be in relationship with. This is true in the big picture (post oak trees, bluebonnet flowers, university traditions) and in the very small (the mulberry tree I climbed as a young girl so I could read my book in its branches). Every place has some essential spirit, but sometimes it goes into hiding. Sometimes it needs a gardener's help to bring it more fully into view. Do you live in an English Tudor–style house? Then a formal knot garden of boxwood shrubs helps tell that story and helps evoke the spirit of an ancient English place. Do you live in a hot and dry climate? Don't pretend otherwise with irrigated lawn grass, but embrace the Mediterranean glory of a rosemary or lavender hedge. Your garden is part of a larger context, a larger story. Rather than fighting that, you can embrace it with your planting choices, and in this way you can help your family and your neighbors to better know the place where they live.

The patch of ground on which you garden exists nowhere else in the world. And you are its caretaker. As my friend, the garden designer Julie Witmer, likes to say, "The goal of gardening is not a perfect place. It's a beloved place." My hometown was not obviously lovable. The journalist could not see its appeal. But despite all the flaws of our beloved, we had made it lovable with our living.

HOW TO MAKE NEW PLANTS IN WATER

1. Snip a few stems or sprigs. The kindest cut for the plant is just *above* a leaf node (area where leaves are growing out of the stem). I look for vigorously growing stems that are not flowering.

2. Remove extra leaves. With scissors or a sharp, clean knife, remove all leaves along the stem except for a few at the top. You want enough green leaves left to keep the cutting alive but not so many leaves that the stem can't support itself and wilts or dies back.

3. Recut the bottom of your stem just *below* a leaf node. This is the point of the stem that has the most natural rooting hormone.

4. Plunge your cuttings into a jar of water and keep in a bright spot for three to four weeks.

5. Pot your rooted cuttings into loose, fluffy potting soil once a good bunch of roots have begun to grow. You want roots that are at least an inch or two long. As long as the leaves aren't wilting, you can keep the roots growing in water to give the cutting a better chance of establishing in soil. If any flowers start to grow, pinch them out.

6. Plants that root well in water include pothos, coleus, begonia, basil, mint, lemon balm, oregano, and plectranthus. Rooting cuttings in water typically works best for plants with soft, green stems, but even woody plants like rosemary can root in water if you choose fresh, soft growth.

PART TWO

GARDENS GROW CONNECTION

I sometimes wonder if all other animals, all plants, maybe even stars and rivers and rocks, dwell in steady awareness of God, while humans alone, afflicted with self-consciousness, imagine ourselves apart.

SCOTT RUSSELL SANDERS, *A PRIVATE HISTORY OF AWE*

A HARVEST
FOR THE BIRDS

The key to success in gardening—and in life—is to be flexible about your goals. One's goal when planting apple trees would seem fairly obvious: apples. More specifically, one's goal is a harvest sufficient for apple crisp, apple pie, applesauce, and—for the truly high achieving—apple cider fresh from the press. So far this fall, I have made both a crisp and a pie, but these were made with apples from a local orchard rather than apples from my backyard trees. Am I a failed orchard keeper? Some might say yes, but I have never been much of a goal setter. I prefer to let life surprise me with success I did not anticipate. It is true that I did not set out to feed my young daughter, her neighborhood playmates, a murder of crows, and a coterie of groundhogs a steady diet of early-autumn apples, but having done so, I count it good, however unanticipated.

No gardener has total control of her garden. She cannot make it rain, she cannot slow the wind, and if she has set out to feed her family with garden produce, then she cannot entirely disinvite the birds from that feast. A U-pick farm not far from my home grows all its cherry trees inside an enormous net-covered enclosure to protect the cherry crop from birds. Many of my Amish neighbors grow blueberries inside chain-link "blueberry tunnels" for the same reason. Here at Maplehurst, I have been known to lay a sheet of black plastic netting, sold under the rather sad name *Bird-X*, over my strawberries, but everything else is fair game. The birds at Maplehurst feast on a steady diet of mulberries (which I developed a taste for in childhood), apples, peaches, and, yes, even the cherries that do still dangle once each year from our lone remaining antique cherry tree.

When the Hebrew Scriptures were penned long ago, there was certainly no such thing as store-bought plastic netting. Harvesting in those days was much less efficient than it is today, yet the wisdom of the Scriptures required that the Israelites take care to harvest even *less* efficiently than they might otherwise have done. In the book of Leviticus they were commanded to leave an unharvested margin in every field of grain. If grain fell to the ground, they were not to gather it up again. And in a vineyard, the owner was allowed to harvest only the first ripe grapes, leaving those that ripened later for others. All of these commands allowed for the practice of gleaning, in which the poor were given access to the sustenance of the land and encouraged, through their own labor, to gather its bounty. I have a strong suspicion the birds showed up too. I doubt the fallen grain went unnoticed by birds roosting in nearby trees, and though they are not mentioned in Leviticus, other Scriptures testify to God's care for these tiny, hungry creatures. In the Gospel of Matthew, Jesus tells his disciples that our heavenly Father "feeds" the birds, though they do not sow, or reap, or store away in barns (Matthew 6:26). If God feeds the birds, who am I to chase them all away? And is a garden without birds, without birdsong, even the garden I want to grow?

Our own goals are often too narrow. We imagine one good thing, like a harvest of strawberries or apples, and we become narrow-minded in our pursuit of it. But the goodness of God is never a rigid, boundaried thing. It is a fountain, a flood, a rain that falls on everything and everyone. As gardeners, we can lean into that, or we can fight it. Personally, I have made this reality my invitation to plant more of the food crops I love. Though I began to garden for me and for my family—planting strawberries, blackberries, peaches, and figs—I have grown into a gardener who also plants for the birds and the bees and the butterflies.

Common milkweed may be poisonous to me, but it is the only food for Monarch butterfly larvae. The bright berries of winterberry and viburnum are not good food for humans, but they are beautiful to the eye, and they feed our birds well. I am sometimes tempted to remove all of the anise hyssop from my flower garden—it has a tendency to take over—but the bees and other pollinating insects love it so much I haven't the heart to pull all of it out.

What kind of gleaning is needed today? Some of our neighbors do still hunger. To our shame, in two thousand years we have not figured out how to share our food so everyone has enough. It is more than possible to work a full-time job and still not have the funds for rent *and* for groceries. We can tithe a portion of our garden produce to a local food bank. We can share our harvest with neighbors. We can volunteer in a community garden that helps feed the hungry. And we can recognize that as populations grow and more wild places are developed for housing and shopping centers and highways, our own gardens may be the only places left for feeding birds. How can we sustain our smallest coinhabitants in the garden that is planet Earth? I will not wag my finger and admonish you to plant only for the birds and butterflies and bees. Instead, I will give you a glimpse into my own garden where my narrow wish to grow food has bubbled up and over into a fountain of buzzing, singing, joy-filled *life*. I will gladly pay the price for that abundant life in mulberries and apples and figs.

CREEPY, CRAWLY
WONDERS

On social media, a friend of mine recently shared an award-winning photo of an ant. Because the photo was taken with the help of a microscope, the magnified image was unrecognizable as that of a garden-variety, picnic-invading ant. When I first scrolled past the photo, I assumed the monster I saw had something to do with the approach of Halloween. When I read the caption more closely, all I could think was that we don't have eyes capable of seeing the face of an ant for a reason. If we could truly see the thing crawling toward our picnic basket, would we ever picnic again? Having now viewed the horror of that magnified image, I assure you, we would not.

And yet there are many ways of seeing. The microscope provides one way. The work of gardening provides another. I am a highly sensitive, squeamish person by anyone's standards. To this day, the sight of anything that scurries and has a tail—even if it is as cute as a Beatrix Potter character—sends me into paroxysms of horrified shivering. And I nearly had a heart attack once when the soil of a container plant I was transplanting into my garden suddenly erupted and revealed in my hand the wrinkled, reptilian face of an enormous toad. I can still feel the shock of that sudden encounter like a quaking in my bones. The only creepy-crawlies I ever made friends with as a child were the little roly-poly bugs that curled up like miniature armadillos. They played dead in a way we found hilarious as children. They reminded us of younger siblings who joined our games of hide-and-seek by standing quite still and covering their own eyes, as if we could not see them because they could not see us.

I hope I have made my squeamish bona fides clear, because I want you to understand the enormity of the change years of gardening have wrought in me. Today, if an earthworm were to wriggle up and onto my hand, I would not shudder. I would not scream. I would feel only mild surprise and a deep gratitude that my garden soil is healthy enough for a community of worms. Thanks to gardening, I have grown to feel more at peace with the icky and the sticky and the creepy and the crawly. It is a miracle, my friends, as astonishing as the harvest of the first pumpkin I ever grew from a seed myself.

Where there was enmity, now there is peace. However true, such phrasing sounds pompous where earthworms and toads are concerned. "So what?" I can imagine my teenagers asking me. "What does it matter if bugs make me scream?" It matters so much more than most of us know. A world without humans, a world without us, is a possible thing. No one would be present to observe the workings of the world, but the workings of the world—from photosynthesis to tides to seasons—would continue like fine clockwork without us. Yet a world without insects would quickly collapse. They can live just fine without us, but we, it turns out, cannot live without them. Can you imagine a world without snakes? Without vultures? Don't do it. Such a world would be a nightmare no encounter with a snake could ever match.

Perhaps it is a matter of perspective. Perhaps we have focused on our small, personal nightmares and refused to consider the nightmare of a world without worms, without snakes, without bees. Not long after we moved into this old farmhouse, we spotted a black snake sunning itself against the warm stones of our home's foundation. A quick Google search told us the black snake was an eastern rat snake, so-called because of its preferred diet. That same Google

search told us we were lucky to have such a snake in and around our home. The snake would be more scared of us than we of him, and an adult rat snake would ensure we never had a rodent problem. That knowledge is the only thing that kept me sane the day I went down into our dirt-floored basement in search of some box or other. I kept my eyes on the ground as I always did, determined not to be taken by surprise if something slithered in a corner. That is why I did not see the snakeskin draped from a pipe above my head. For a half second, I imagined I had walked right into a snake hanging from the basement ceiling. My relief at seeing it was only a shed snakeskin was soon tempered by the realization that the skin was evidence our snake did sometimes dangle from the ceiling pipes. Fortunately, the only thing I dislike more than the slither of a snake is the scurry of a mouse's tail. We took no steps to rid our basement of the snake, but from then on I would only go downstairs with my hands held out in front of my face, and my eyes roving up, down, up, down.

Making peace with wild things doesn't require that we hold hands with them or call them cute. All that is required is that we understand them. And that we appreciate them. And that we give thanks for them—even if we prefer to keep them at arm's length. The truth is that we need them, for the beauty and the flourishing of our earth relies on them. We have no flowers without them. We have no food without them. We have no *life* without them. I don't really understand why we begin as enemies. No one ever taught me to fear rats or snakes, and I am sure I never taught my daughter to abhor even the sight of a spider. If anything, I read *Charlotte's Web* to her and told her that every house needs a spider to keep the other bug populations under control. Perhaps our squeamishness and our fear are wounds in need of healing. Perhaps they are a symptom of some brokenness that cries out for restoration. If so, the garden is the place that heals us and restores a good and right connection with the teeny, tiny, scurrying life that sustains our world.

BUTTERFLY AND PLANT PAIRS

*While adult butterflies can feed on many nectar sources, their larvae (baby butterflies!) have narrower diets, and may even be limited to a single so-called host plant. Here is a list of host plants and the butterflies they support in my mid-Atlantic region. I hope this list inspires you to research the appropriate host plants for your garden. Keep in mind that these plants will be **food** for caterpillars. We should be thrilled when our pesticide-free plants show signs of leaf munching.*

1. **Monarch:** milkweed varieties (*Asclepius*)

2. **Pipevine swallowtail:** pipevines (*Aristolochia*)

3. **Zebra swallowtail:** pawpaws (*Asimina triloba*)

4. **Black swallowtail:** parsley family (parsley, dill, carrot, Queen Anne's lace)

5. **Eastern tiger swallowtail:** tulip tree (*Liriodendron tulipifera*), wild black cherry (*Prunus serotina*), and ash (*Fraxinus*)

6. **Spicebush swallowtail:** spicebush (*Lindera benzoin*) and sassafras (*Sassafras albidum*)

7. **Variegated fritillary:** violets and pansies

RAINING DOGS AND CATS AND CHICKENS

I am not really an animal person, and yet somehow in middle age, I have found myself making a home with one dog, two cats, and a baker's dozen of chickens. The dog I blame on the children and British television gardener Monty Don. My older son begged for a dog of his own for two straight years, but his dog allergy kept me firm in my resolve until we realized he never became sick around his grandparents' hypoallergenic cockapoo, Sophie. Resolve tumbled quite quickly after that, in part because the UK's favorite gardener, Monty Don, made dogs seem as natural and as needed in the garden as terra-cotta pots and boxwood.

The cats and the chickens are easily explainable because they are so useful. Although I understand there is some controversy around the keeping of cats outdoors (one murdered songbird is one too many), the previous owners of our farmhouse assured us we needed a barn cat or two to keep the mice population down. Mice in my kitchen is a nightmare no amount of Beatrix Potter pastel watercolors have ever cured in me, so we acquired two barn cats soon after moving in. I am not convinced they do much besides sun themselves on the gravel of our outdoor patio, but it is true that I have never yet in ten years found a mouse in my kitchen.

The chickens are the most utilitarian members of our menagerie. They give us brilliant orange yolks for our breakfasts in exchange for pellet feed and the occasional Halloween pumpkin scraps. They also give me excellent manure for my compost pile. I have even been known to dig out some of the manure-rich soil found in their enclosed run to add to my planting holes for new roses. Visiting children and my brother-in-law Mike always beg to collect the eggs each morning (Mike calls it "picking eggs"), and I find myself telling the parents and Mike's wife, my sister, that chickens really are the easiest animals you can keep. Unlike most children, they even put themselves to bed each night, as if the setting sun triggers some internal alarm clock they can't ignore.

Yet as much as I try to rationalize how a nonanimal person might find herself participating in the care of so many animals, the truest answer must be not that my son was adorable and irresistible in his begging, nor that my fear of mice trumps all else, but rather that I am a gardener. Gardeners are in the business of tending life. The longer you garden, the less able you are to draw narrow boundaries around the kind of life you want to tend. At first, you might say yes to roses and no to aphids, but when you discover that aphids are food for ladybugs and ladybugs are almost as lovely as roses, well, you put down the poison sprays and decide to grow roses *and* ladybugs. And that's how it begins. Life is always connected to life. Species cannot thrive in isolation. And the wise and experienced gardener draws her boundary lines and puts up her fences very carefully.

But even the wise gardener has her patience tested. Though I have never yet seen it on an episode of *Gardeners' World*, I suspect that even Monty Don has lost some special plant to the digging of a much-loved dog. The chickens have often been the culprits in my own garden. They love nothing more than freshly turned earth, which is wonderful if they attack a new planting bed, breaking up clods of dirt, but terrible if they discover freshly laid mulch. One chicken can scatter a blanket of neat mulch faster than you can say "soup," which is a terrible thing to say about a lovely bird that gives so much in return for its safekeeping. I have never made soup from a mulch-destroying bird, but I have kept them penned up in spring when the plants have not yet grown in to cover the ground. I do try

to make their prison as comfortable as possible by feeding them bucketloads of weeds. And let that be reason number 99 to keep chickens in a garden: a welcoming place for weeds!

When I insist that gardeners tend life and animals bring more life to a place, I hope you understand that this one word—*life*—holds an abundance. It holds surprises. It holds everything good. Because I am not a natural animal lover, I have never named a chicken as if it were a pet. But when my friend's daughter comes to my garden, suddenly I am not only a chicken keeper, but I am keeper of Betsy and Matilda and Henrietta. And just like that, more life. Also, more laughter. We gardeners are often inspired to begin because we love roses or zucchini or little cucumbers that look like miniature watermelons. But even a small dose of love for life will multiply, and before you know it a broody hen has hatched a clutch of eggs, a neighbor child has set up an acorn store under the fig tree, and a cat sits suspiciously staring up into the hawthorn tree, alerting you to a perfect nest with three perfect china-blue eggs.

It's true that I am still not an animal person. I am a gardener. But in addition to dinosaur kale and David Austin roses, I grow cute chicks, and childhood play, and birds opening wide for worms, and a puppy whose curly coat is a beautiful echo of the maple leaves in fall. And to think, when I began, all I wanted was a homegrown tomato. Aren't gardens miraculous?

CHICKENS IN THE GARDEN

I think every garden should have a flock of chickens nearby,
even though the two (chicken and garden) don't always get along.
Here is how I help my chickens help my garden:

1. Chickens can help control insect populations. I especially appreciate that chickens love to eat ticks.

2. Chickens can scatter fresh mulch and compost faster than you can say "shoo." I keep my flock penned up until the perennials have grown in enough to cover the mulch. A flock of smaller hens, called bantams, will also be less destructive in an ornamental garden.

3. An enclosed chicken run is a great place for discarding our weeds.

4. Chicken manure is excellent garden food as long as we don't layer it around our plants while it is still hot and fresh. Chicken manure that has sat and decomposed for at least a few months—and preferably a year—is garden gold. If mixed into a high-heat compost pile, it will be safe to use much more quickly.

5. Chickens are easy to keep and bring so much life to our gardens. They give us eggs, they give us fertilizer, they give us delight.

MAKING FRIENDS WITH
THE NEIGHBORS

This fall, the backyard show that no blockbuster could compete with arrived via shaky iPhone video as I tried, day after day, to capture the hilarity of a groundhog family feasting on fallen apples. Throw in my daughter, the young twins from next door, and a rickety stepladder from my husband's tool shed, and the entertainment value was consistently high. The girls dangled from one small tree, picking green apples I felt sure would make their tummies ache, while a groundhog mother shook the limbs of another low-growing tree to feed her brood fresh fruit. Instead of grabbing the apples and running off with them in their mouths, as I expected, the groundhog family spent hours every day standing upright on their haunches in the dappled sunshine beneath the orchard trees nibbling apples right down to the seed and stem.

I have been at war with these groundhogs and their kin since first beginning to garden here at Maplehurst. Before I even knew their name—what were those enormous furry creatures that scurried away into half-hidden tunnels at the sight of us?—I considered them my enemies. Our enmity was sealed the summer the peach tree my father had planted for me finally grew fruit. A few days before the peaches were quite ready for picking, a groundhog, determined to claim those fragrant fruits for himself, ripped an entire limb from my poor little peach tree.

In that moment, I could have murdered him. My sense of his cuteness evaporated, and I saw only a destroyer of trees.

My antipathy toward our resident groundhogs reached a new low when I discovered a love for dahlias. The first summer I planted dahlias in my new flower garden, I watched those green plants grow all summer long. They grew tall. They leafed out. I couldn't wait for the first flowers to emerge in late summer, but before I could pick even one bouquet, some groundhog came in the night and tore my plants to shreds. I want to grow dahlias. I want to harvest peaches. I do not work so hard only to spread a fruit and salad buffet for groundhog colonies. And so, like many gardeners before me, I wage war with unorthodox weapons: fences, pepper spray, plastic netting, plants in the onion family. The dahlia-eating groundhog did me a favor in the end: I planted garlic chives in the back areas of my flower garden hoping to deter him and discovered a new favorite cottage garden flower. These perennial,

flowering herbs, it turns out, are not only beautiful, but their fresh white flowers arrive in late summer just when everything else in the flower garden has grown tired. They are a gift at a time when everything else is faded and sad, and I would never have planted them if it weren't for my groundhog enemy.

Gardening with animal neighbors is a constant give and take. The deer give moments of joy, for instance when they bring their young fawns to shelter in the shrubs behind our house. The groundhogs gave laughter and delight, eating their windfalls in plain sight of my kitchen window. For a whole season, we marveled at the frequent visits of a perfectly white squirrel. And could there be anything sweeter than the baby rabbit who took shelter from the rain beneath lettuces that had grown beyond the frame of a raised bed? And yet the deer munched down an entire row of small eastern white pines I had planted on the western boundary of our garden. I have already catalogued the groundhogs' crimes. The squirrels have been known to dig up freshly planted flower plugs in spring and bulbs in fall. And, of course, even the tiniest bunnies can stretch themselves up to nibble lettuce and Swiss chard plants down to a nub.

The taking is often easiest to see. When tree bark is rubbed raw or dahlias are torn down, the cost is easy to tally and enmity grows. But the giving is harder to observe. What trees have been planted by busy squirrels carrying acorns, seeds, and nuts? How many roots from how many plants have received much-needed oxygen because a groundhog tunneled through compacted soil? How many fast-growing weeds are kept under control by a rabbit's grazing? If gardening has taught me anything, it has taught me how much I don't know, don't see, and don't understand. The environment my garden is a part of has begun to seem more mysterious and more complex the more time I have spent observing it. New gardeners are reckless with nets and traps and sprays. And I have been that gardener. Still am on many days. Experienced gardeners have been humbled by so many seasons spent observing and participating in the miracle of interconnected life.

Experienced gardeners are sometimes quick to act (when you know a noxious weed through experience, you go after it at first sight), but they are also slow to act, aware that every action lands in a garden like a stone tossed into a pond.

As I write this essay, I have not resolved my feelings toward my groundhog neighbors. I worry about the holes they dig that could break a human leg. I worry for my newly planted trees. I will go on plugging the tunnel exits in the gravel foundation beneath my garden shed so that groundhogs have no easy access to my flower garden. But I have spent too much time with them by now to feel only mistrust and dislike. Time and proximity have a way of softening our perceptions of an enemy. I felt genuine grief and guilt when a groundhog ran too near the tire of my husband's truck as he rushed down the driveway toward some appointment or other. Life is so very *alive*, who am I to wish for death? Especially the death of an animal whose life and purpose and contribution to the world I can hardly begin to know. Perhaps the only way is to hold all of the contradictions at once. I will go on rolling large stones into inconvenient tunnels. I will spread garlic chive seeds where I want to protect other flowers (of course, thanks to the wind, these vigorous spreaders generally go plant themselves where *they* will, not I). And I will take time to observe my neighbors. I will give thanks that my garden is no static, sterile place, but rather busy and bustling and altogether beyond my control.

ORNAMENTAL FOOD

In a flourishing garden, divisions and enmities dissolve, including the distinction between ornamental and edible. Here are plants that fulfill both sides of that equation with beauty and good taste:

1. **Lacinato kale** (also called Tuscan or dinosaur kale, *Brassica oleracea*): This is my favorite kale to eat and to see in my garden; the leaves are fairly flat, which makes them easy to prepare in the kitchen and beautifully sculptural in the garden.

2. **Alpine strawberries** (also called fraises des bois, *Fragaria vesca*): A nearly wild European strawberry, this highly ornamental and highly delicious strawberry makes a great edging plant in the garden and looks wonderful in containers filling in the gaps beneath larger plants; it is also easy to grow from seed.

3. **Swiss chard** (*Beta vulgaris*): With green leaves that can be cooked like spinach and bright stems that can be cooked or even pickled, Swiss chard can withstand the heat of the summer garden while bringing excitement with its bright, multicolored stems. Choose a variety like 'Five Color Silverbeet' for stems in red, orange, and yellow or 'Fordhook Giant' for a cool green and white color combination.

4. **Purple basil** ('Dark Opal' basil, *Ocimum basilicum*): Every cook loves basil, but even the flower arrangers will love this deep purple basil with small lavender flowers; purple basil tastes great, brightens up salads, looks very ornamental in a garden bed, and provides wonderful filler for special bouquets.

5. **Nasturtium** (*Tropaeolum*): With many varieties to choose from, nasturtium can grow as petite container plants or sprawling garden vines; either way, their distinctive, bright flowers and round green leaves add a peppery bite and festive beauty to summer salads.

SHARING
THE GARDEN

Today, I garden with deer, groundhogs, cats, and chickens, but I once gardened with other human beings. In fact, I first became a gardener because, while living on the South Side of Chicago, a graduate school friend invited me and a few others to help her tend a small plot in a community garden near campus. Her invitation astonished me. I knew nothing about how to keep a vegetable garden, had never given the idea of it any thought at all, and only knew it as a hobby my father enjoyed in Texas. I wasn't even sure I liked the fruits of a typical vegetable garden. When I was growing up, my father always had a small "relish" plate near his own dinner plate with sliced, homegrown tomato, cucumber, and onion. He clearly *relished* those flavors, but I was fairly sure I did not.

I said yes to my friend despite my misgivings, and the summer before my first child was born in September was spent tending tomatoes, basil, and lettuces. We were not very successful gardeners in those days. Our plot never flourished like some of the adjoining ones did, and by August we generally had more weeds than anything else, but I have never forgotten how my friend celebrated our daughter's arrival by bringing us a bowl of pasta salad made with our own cherry tomatoes and basil. Probably it was the accomplishment I tasted in that pasta salad that kept me returning to that same community garden summer after summer. Our daughter learned to use a watering can there. The son born three years after loved to run up and down the rows that separated one plot from another. Fourteen years later, he still has a small scar on his forehead, earned when he fell and cut his head against a stone someone had placed to mark the corner of their bed.

That shared garden marked me—changed me—as surely as it left its mark on my son. But in what ways, exactly, was I changed? If I never did learn how to keep a perfect plot, if I always was embarrassed to visit my garden in late summer lest someone else connect me with those toppled tomato vines mixed with weeds, what did I gain exactly? Beyond an annual bowl of pasta salad? While my primary memory of that garden is guilt over my lack of knowledge and my failure to weed with consistency, I also remember the thrill of our first visit each spring. The wind was always a little too cold, and we sometimes planted our tomatoes before the soil had properly warmed, but we were almost bursting with hope and happiness at the end of another long Midwestern winter. No wonder my little boy was always running. Over the years we gardened there, our annual ritual of spring planting began to seem like an absolutely necessary way to mark the passing of winter and the nearness of summer. That we spread our bare hands in good, dark earth every year enabled me, I think, to go on living in that dense urban environment. I loved that city, and I loved living there, but every human needs bodily contact with the life of our planet.

While I often shied away from the community aspects of our community garden out of guilt or shame, gardening alongside others was an invaluable way to learn. At the same time, it gave me access—beyond my memories of my father—to a vision of a life spent nearer to the soil. Keeping a garden began to seem possible. Even a new gardener like myself, with more questions than answers, could grow a delicious bowl of summer salad. And in a culture in which we often relate to other people only along narrow lines of affinity—church membership, perhaps, or the workplace—a community garden opened up so many new connections with people I might never otherwise talk to or learn from or befriend. Our

South Side community garden was a place where the divisions of race or religion, town or gown, still existed, but they ceased to be the primary lens through which we viewed one another. Instead, here was the person who grew the best tomatoes. Here was the one who knew how to grow garlic. Here was the neighbor who understood that our shared garden needed a large table set beneath the shade of a centrally planted tree.

We have this idea of gardening as a deeply solitary activity, like Beatrix Potter's Mr. McGregor hoeing cabbages and chasing the bunnies till they squeeze beneath the garden gate. Instead, we cannot keep a garden well without the participation and support of a whole cast of living things, from fungi and earthworms to bees and birds. And no gardener is quite as solitary as she imagines herself to be. Either she needs someone willing to bake bread with all of her extra zucchini or she needs someone—at least occasionally—to admire the first flush of roses in bloom. Whether we garden in cities or rural places or somewhere in between, gardens connect us to one another. And most of us would not even have begun gardening if we had never observed someone else doing it or had not been invited in by a friend, a neighbor, or a friendly grower at the local outdoor market.

Shame separates us and keeps us apart. It used to keep me away from my urban garden in August so that the weeds of which I was ashamed only grew worse. The ghost of every houseplant we've ever neglected or outright killed can build up in us a certainty that our thumbs are not "green" and that we would only embarrass ourselves if we tried something ambitious in our backyard. But actual gardening—even the simple, small first step—breaks down our separation and our shame. We reach out with questions. We reach out with pasta salad. Impossible things begin to seem possible. We, too, can learn to grow garlic. We, too, can learn to love the taste of a freshly sliced and salted tomato. When we begin to garden, we grow plants and we grow connection: to our place, to other forms of life, and to our neighbors. It is a better harvest even than zucchini.

PLANTS THE DEER
DO NOT CARE TO SHARE

We can't share all our garden plants with the local deer, or we won't have a garden left to share with neighbors. Here are North American native perennials that deer generally avoid. There are no guarantees, however. Haven't you munched on something you didn't really like when you were very hungry?

False Indigo (*Baptisia*)
Members of the legume family, these stately shrubs can help enrich our garden soil. The flowers are similar to those of sweet pea. 'Purple Smoke' is a special variety named among the top-ten baptisias by Delaware's Mt. Cuba Center in one of its esteemed plant trials.

Coneflower (*Echinacea purpurea*)
Plants traditionally used medicinally, like echinacea, are often plants the deer ignore. Coneflowers have strong, daisylike flowers that look equally at home in prairie gardens and cottage gardens.

Gaura (*Gaura lindheimeri*)
Also called beeblossom, this is one of my favorite American native perennials for sunny, dry corners of the garden and for containers. I love

to watch these birdlike flowers dance on the tips of their wiry stems whenever the breeze picks up. 'Whirling Butterflies' is a pale and pretty variety.

Goldenrod (*Solidago*)
A common sight in wild areas of the Northeast as summer turns to fall, some goldenrod varieties make great ornamental, deer-resistant, pollinator-friendly garden plants. I love the woodland goldenrod called zigzag (*Solidago flexicaulis*) in my own garden. This is also a host plant for several types of small moths.

Beebalm (*Monarda bradburiana*)
Butterflies love this member of the mint family. The aromatic leaves can even be used in teas. I love the unique fuzzy, globular shape of the flower, which contrasts with more typical flower shapes.

PART THREE

GARDENS
GROW
WHOLENESS

❖◆❖◆❖◆❖

*If you wish to make anything grow, you must understand it,
and understand it in a very real sense. "Green fingers"
are a fact, and a mystery only to the unpracticed. But green
fingers are the extensions of a verdant heart.*

RUSSELL PAGE, *THE EDUCATION OF A GARDENER*

A HODGEPODGE
AND A MISHMASH

W hen I was a little girl growing up in Texas, I answered every adult's favorite question with a single word: *artist*. I wanted to be an artist when I grew up. I'm not sure what I meant by that word exactly. For Halloween one year, I dressed up like my idea of an artist—a red beret, a paintbrush and palette, a white dress shirt of my father's for a smock—but it wasn't as if I used a paintbrush very often. Right about the time of the Halloween costume, I had graduated from the ease of Crayola markers to the ease of watercolor pencils. Later, perhaps recognizing that I lacked skill with a paintbrush, I began telling everyone in my life I wanted to be an interior designer when I grew up. That idea was later buried under an interest in architecture, which would itself lie buried under a lack of interest in mathematics and a strong interest in poetry. So I set my colored pencils aside and studied literature. There is still an artist in me, and there is a designer, too, but ten years of place-making and garden-making at Maplehurst have revealed to me that more than either of those, I am at heart a collector. This is not good news for either my home or my garden.

I'm not sure anyone is born a collector, as such. I think I was born with an eye for unique or pretty things. We become collectors because one more special thing is always beckoning. At three years old, I carried a collection of pretty

pebbles stuffed inside the little pillow cover I carried like a hybrid purse/blanket. I vividly recall the Sunday morning when the zipper on my pillow cover broke, and my precious collection spilled across the carpet beneath the pews of my grandmother's church. By the time I exited kindergarten, I knew that one scratch-and-sniff sticker was fun (I loved strawberry and loved to hate dill pickle), but a whole album of stickers with pages dedicated to scratch-and-sniff, puffy, and rainbow stickers was even better. In the mid-1980s, I collected china thimbles, of all things, and even had a small wooden display case for them. I distinctly remember a white china thimble decorated with a tiny painted portrait of a Texas bluebonnet flower. Other collections included marbles, miniatures, and even—very briefly—the collectible that probably spawned all other world collectibles: stamps.

The instinct to collect, though it might lead to vast numbers of objects, is a preoccupation with the part rather than the whole. A collector gathers a

collection because the collector's gaze is always zoomed in on the singularity of something wonderful. The big picture (*Do I need one more? Do I have room for one more?*) fades quickly when the collector spies some unique and lovely thing. As a home decorator, I have always fed my hunger for collecting with regular visits to thrift stores and antique stores. Lately, I have discovered the thrill of online auctions run by a local estate-sale auction business. This has been a very exciting and slightly dangerous discovery. Recent oddball home acquisitions include a brass trivet with legs designed to keep a hot teakettle well away from the tea table, a small brass box shaped like a treasure chest, a framed botanical print of a tulip poplar tree, and a ceramic vase with a three-dimensional ceramic honeybee on its rim. Such small treasures are easy to bring home without upsetting the balance of my interior design, but I have also been known to bring home rugs, chairs, and tables that must then be crammed into some corner or other. The result is often a hodgepodge rather than a cohesive design. Instead of asking myself, "What does this space need?" I ask, "Where is there room for this delightful new thing?"

Unfortunately, my approach is much the same in my garden. Sometimes, this works out rather well. When my good friend Meghan of Nomad Farm hosted a plant sale in my backyard, I eagerly claimed a white-flowering North American native wisteria called 'Nivea' left over at the end of the sale, though I had no idea where I would plant it. I knew 'Nivea' was a very special plant, and Meghan was offering it at a great price. The collector in me bought it, and the designer in me convinced my husband to quickly rig up a steel hook and cable trellis around the French doors that connect our kitchen and our back garden. The wisteria grew by leaps over the summer months, twining itself beautifully around the cables to climb the wall without directly clinging to it, and my designer self has thanked my collector self many times since then.

Generally though, my urge to collect does nothing for my garden's design. When I bring home one of everything from the local garden center, my home's exterior begins to look as much a hodgepodge as my home's interior. If it were only a matter of style, it might not matter, but it is difficult for the mind and body—even the mind and body of a collector—to feel at peace in a mishmash and a hodgepodge. Even the collector longs for cohesiveness. Even the collector longs for wholeness. Or perhaps it is the artist in me who longs for such things. Perhaps the collector in me and the artist in me need one another. This division within myself—between collector and designer—might just be a saving grace.

My designer self and my collector self continue their sometimes fruitful, sometimes frustrating tug-of-war. Because I collect garden plants, I now have experience growing many different garden plants. Because I do still love great design, I do not hesitate to dig out, compost, or give away plants that are not pulling their visual weight in the garden. Though gardening from a divided self feels like a tug-of-war, I hope that it will one day feel like a melting pot. Where there was tension, let there be harmony. Where there was conflict, may there be cooperation. I might still be struggling for consistency and wholeness in my designs, but I have at least learned that the problem is not *out there* in my garden but *in here* in my own head and heart. What is a garden, after all, but simply a place that is cared for by a gardener? If I can learn to garden with my whole self, I feel sure my garden will grow more whole. Meanwhile, with my full self, I am taking joy in the triumph of the wisteria. It is a collector's treasure and a designer's dream. May it live a long and floriferous life.

A TEA GARDEN

A garden designed around a theme is perfect for the gardener who is also a collector, and what could be more refreshing than a tea garden? While a true cup of tea is made with leaves from the tea plant, Camellia sinensis, which is only hardy in zones 8 through 11, numerous plants make wonderful herbal and floral drinks called tisanes.

Anise Hyssop (*Agastache foeniculum*)

The tall flowering plant bees love in my garden makes a naturally sweet, licorice-flavored tea. Note that anise hyssop is native to North America and is not the same as the hyssop native to Europe.

German Chamomile (*Matricaria chamomilla*)

This annual from the daisy family is used to make the classic herbal tea for relaxation. Chamomile is easily confused with feverfew (*Tanacetum parthenium*), but the former is more fragrant.

Edible Hibiscus (*Hibiscus sabdariffa*)

The nonhardy, edible form of hibiscus can be grown in pots and brought indoors for colder winters.

Lemon Verbena (*Aloysia triphylla*)

This is the one for those who love citrus-flavored teas. As with many herbs, harvest leaves frequently to encourage young, fresh growth.

Mint

No matter the variety you choose—from spearmint to peppermint to mojito mint and more—all mints should be grown in containers as they will spread aggressively.

New Jersey Tea (*Ceanothus americanus*)

A compact shrub with clusters of white flowers, this is a host plant for spring azure and summer azure butterflies. During the American Revolution, the leaves of this plant were used instead of imported teas. Whether you make tea with it or reserve it for the hummingbirds, this one is a must for an American tea-themed garden.

NATIVE PLANTS
AND KINDNESS

Every time I return home to this redbrick farmhouse, I point my car down an almost perfect example of whole and coherent design. More than a century ago, the long driveway that stretches from the road to the front porch was planted with a double row of maple trees. It isn't a sophisticated or subtle design, but it is a strong statement and easy to read even from within a swiftly passing car. The design is, of course, comprised of living things—trees—and living things all become dead or dying things in time. Because these two long, parallel rows were planted all at once, the effect of the grand symmetrical design has only grown visually stronger over the decades. But sadly, trees that begin their lives together also generally end their lives together. Our design isn't fading, it is failing, and it is failing swiftly and all at once.

I am seeking a kind of visual wholeness in my garden, the kind I see in the old driveway design, but that is not the only form wholeness can take. Visual wholeness is a superficial cohesiveness, though I don't mean to invoke the negative connotation of that word. By *superficial* I mean only that this coherence lies on the surface of things. But wholeness can touch much more deeply than that. The old maple trees that yet remain in matched pairs on either side of our driveway still offer a vision of wholeness, but the vision is skin deep. Literally. Most of our old trees have been hollowed out by age, and every storm threatens to bring them down. After ten years of living here at Maplehurst, we really only have a few trees left from the original driveway planting, and those that remain have been slowly whittled away by wind and rain. A new design and a new vision have become critical, but I have struggled to come up with ideas that feel right and whole all the way down and all the way through. I want a plan for that portion of our property that doesn't just appear to be whole but *is* whole. I want trees and shrubs and plants that not only make a visual impact but make an impact, full stop.

The plants best adapted to support whole, flourishing life in our gardens are usually our native species. While my maples look cohesive, they are not actually well connected with their surrounding ecosystem. Most of my maples are Norway maples, a non-native tree prized one hundred years ago for its ability to grow quickly but one we now recognize as a quick-growing bully. In the natural woodland areas near my Pennsylvania home, Norway maples are crowding out the native tree species that support more of our native insects and caterpillars. One of my favorite garden writers, Ken Druse, says Norway maples "should never be planted in the United States." These trees are "moisture-guzzling invasive aliens that leaf out earlier and drop their leaves later than local species. They put an allelopathic chemical in the soil that inhibits the growth of other plants, and they produce blackish-green shingle-like leaves creating some of the densest shade of any deciduous tree. Planting beneath them is next to impossible."[2] Visual wholeness is lovely to behold, but does a visual wholeness achieved with "moisture-guzzling" monster trees really count as wholeness? Or is this the horticultural equivalent of an emperor with no clothes?

If my own harsh language has you longing to defend Norway maples, I understand. When one of our oldest and biggest maples recently had to be taken down to make way for a building project, I told myself it was "only" a Norway maple, but I still felt like a murderer.

And this is where the often-heated debates about native plants break down for me. I'm not really interested in demonizing living things. I'd rather celebrate the good things nature offers us. We don't need to call Norway maples names, but if we understand their limitations and weaknesses, we can better appreciate the beauty and strength of our native trees. I was sad to see that large, old maple go, but I am thrilled every time I plant a red maple or a white oak or a tulip poplar or a hawthorn or any one of the native tree species that support so much of our local ecosystem with their seeds, their berries, their leaf litter, and their shade.

I am still feeling my way toward a new design and a new vision for the long driveway here at Maplehurst, one that aims for a larger, deeper kind of wholeness. I recently added a few matched pairs of columnar maples near the entrance at the road, but I have no intention of carrying that small moment of symmetry all the way down the drive. Instead, I'd like to open things up. Where some of the large trees have already come down, I will not fill the gaps with new trees so that the driveway feels less closed off. And I have already begun planting small groves and single statement trees along the edges of the property. There is now a tiny grove of tulip poplar trees planted up on the highest bit of ground. Long before they reach their full forest height, they will nurture finches, cardinals, quail, and even ruby-throated hummingbirds. I planted a sycamore on the lowest area, and I hope the statuesque white limbs one day call to mind a landscape painting by our beloved local artist Andrew Wyeth. I filled out an area of non-native Norway spruce with Washington hawthorn trees. The berries will feed birds in winter and support insects and caterpillars all summer. With so much life to consider, with so many fruitful connections to nurture, what time is left for name-calling and finger-wagging?

SEEDHEADS TO SAVOR

Purple Love Grass (*Eragrostis spectabilis*)

Widespread in North America, this warm-season bunch grass stays fairly small but erupts with a showy, red-tinted cloud in late summer. Butterflies adore it. Perfect for soil that is too dry for lawn.

Coneflower (*Echinacea*)

Purple coneflowers and other echinacea are familiar and much-loved summer flowers. If the flowers are not deadheaded, strong, sculptural seedheads make wonderful winter food for birds.

Sunflower (*Helianthus annuus*)

Annual sunflowers are not only easy to grow from seed, but they can produce many new seeds to feed birds. I grow a few sterile, hybrid sunflowers (like 'Sunfinity') for cutting and bringing indoors, but the larger seed-producing annual sunflowers become wonderful natural bird feeders if left to dry out right in the garden.

Northern Sea Oats or River Oats (*Chasmanthium latifolium*)

This American native grass tolerates shade and produces the most beautiful pale green seedheads in summer. The seeds resemble oats and gradually turn a ruddy bronze color. This perennial, ornamental grass can grow taller than its typical three feet in full sun and spreads via its seeds fairly aggressively. Plant it in an area where you want a spreading ground cover and many happy birds.

Morning Light Maiden Grass (*Miscanthus sinensis* 'Morning Light')

This tall, dense clumping grass looks silvery green until late summer when burgundy inflorescences (they look like feathers!) begin to grow. In winter, these feathery beauties bleach to a pale color but remain as a highlight of the winter landscape, even when dusted with snow. They make great additions to winter wreaths and dried flower arrangements. Plant it with plenty of room to reach its full size because this large grass will not be easily dug and divided.

CONTROLLING THE UNCONTROLLABLE VINE

The pursuit of wholeness in our gardens is a risky venture. Take vines, for example. They are the stuff of fairy tales for a reason, but are they ladders to heaven or the dangerous entrance to a giant's lair? In my first book, *Roots and Sky*, I waxed lyrical about the morning glory vines quietly twining themselves around the spindles of our farmhouse porch. Ten years later, I have just about eradicated those morning glory pests—fee, fie, fo, fum. I rarely jump faster than when I spy two little heart-shaped leaves poking out of the soil near the front door. First, I gasp, next I leap, and then I tug. And that's how I bid adieu to yet another progeny of 'Grandpa Ott's' heirloom morning glory.

They once seemed like such a good and—yes—glorious idea. The previous owners of Maplehurst had nudged the ball rolling. They must have planted morning glory seeds sometime in the spring before our arrival. We moved into the house in August, and when I brought our newest arrival, baby Elsa, home from the hospital in mid-September, morning glory vines had climbed the porch rails high enough to decorate the borders of our first family photograph. And morning glory flowers are truly stunning. The 'Grandpa Ott's' variety I found through the Seed Savers Exchange heirloom seed catalog offers up large, purple trumpet flowers with pale, starry throats. They are like galaxies you can hold in your hand every morning. But the decorous vines of our first year were obviously new introductions to the garden at Maplehurst. Within a few years, and having sown my own seeds (of beautiful destruction?) all around the house, I began to realize that morning glory flowers make seeds, and before you know it, Jack the Giant Killer could use your morning glories to scale porches and rosebushes and you have found yourself a new full-time occupation as a weeder of baby vines.

Well, there's the bad news. As for the good news, did I mention that morning glories look like starry nights? Planted in the right place (perhaps a distant fence or mailbox), morning glory vines are magic. I've never forgotten how my father transformed a chain-link fence on my grandmother's North Texas farm with a simple row of morning glory seeds. Of course, we could decline to take the risk altogether. Whether we are talking about thorny climbing roses that must be tamed while wearing leather gauntlet gloves or the silver lace vine that quickly swallowed the entrance to my flower garden, vines contribute to the visual

wholeness of our gardens precisely because they are so wild and unruly and will do anything to fill the space between ground and sky. Risky but worthwhile.

I treasure vines because they bring a vertical dimension to gardens that are mostly planted out on a horizontal plane. They fill gaps we may not even have noticed were there. In this way, they help us achieve the kind of wholeness that is nearest to the idea of *entire* or *complete*. Chosen with care (though I have only learned to choose well because I have chosen poorly so many times), climbing vines can become the walls—or at least the beautiful wallpaper—of our outdoor rooms. While I regret the morning glories and the silver lace vine, I am quietly optimistic about my recent foray into the world of wisteria. Japanese and Chinese wisterias are beloved for their abundant racemes of purple flowers—like bunches of grapes—but they can become invasive in North America (I recall seeing wisteria vines romping through Virginia roadside forests, which is not at all where they are meant to be). Just as important, these wisteria are very large and very heavy and need serious support. For all these reasons, I never imagined bringing wisteria into the garden at Maplehurst until I was introduced to our native *Wisteria frutescens* varieties like 'Amethyst Falls' and my own 'Nivea'. Now my very own wisteria is twining itself around heavy-duty stainless steel cables attached with eye hooks to the wall around the French doors that lead from our little sunroom to our back garden. The eye hooks and the cable serve a double purpose: they give the wisteria something to which they can cling (which they need, unlike the English ivy invasive in my area that will happily root itself directly onto just about any flat wall), and they keep a bit of air flow between the green leaves and the wood of the wall. If I ever need to remove the vine, I won't have to hack the wall down to do it.

Which is also something I learned the hard way. Didn't I tell you I have made just about all the vine mistakes it is possible to make? One of the most beautiful features of our previous vegetable garden was the white wooden arbor gate at its entrance. I planted a 'New Dawn' climbing rose to grow over that garden gate, and within three years the entrance was crowned by a great tumble of shell-pink roses. The beauty of it was astonishing even for me, the gardener who had first dreamed of it. Except I had made one fatal error: when the rose was still young, small, and pliable, I encouraged the canes to weave in and out of the arbor's latticework sides. It seemed like the obvious thing to do. Wasn't this a climbing rose, after all? But because this was the first serious climbing rose I had ever grown, I had no concept of how to prune such a rose and no idea how large those slim, pliable canes would one day become. Essentially, I had allowed the rose and the latticework to become almost a unity, and I left myself no way to prune out old or diseased canes without practically tearing apart the lattice. *Whoopsie.* Essentially, I gave up on pruning, I handed the arbor over to that vigorous but beautiful rose, and when the whole garden came out to make way for a new driveway, I vowed never to repeat my mistake. Now I tie in all climbing roses with twine, rather than allow them to weave in and out of their support.

If you want a garden you can easily control, by all means, garden in two dimensions. Grow grass and do nothing to bridge the space between smooth lawn and tall tree. A garden that is allowed—even encouraged—to grow up and down and all around is a wild thing. You might find yourself pushing pale pink roses away from your eyes. You might find yourself rocking on a front porch that looks like it belongs to the enchanted home of Sleeping Beauty. You might spy a few heart-shaped leaves and wonder that nuisance weeds can be so beautiful. It is a garden paradox I am always hoping to solve. It is also a garden paradox I am glad I have not yet solved, for a garden we do not fully control is a wonderful thing.

WELL-BEHAVED VINES
AND CLIMBERS

'Zéphirine Drouhin' Climbing Rose
The most polite climbing rose I know
is an heirloom rose introduced in
1868. 'Zéphirine Drouhin' is virtually
thornless, which makes pruning a
joy. The flowers are deep rosy-pink
and smell wonderfully fruity. This
rose prefers warmer climates (probably no colder than my own zone 6
garden) and is sometimes bothered
by diseases like black spot. I have
two planted some distance from my
house, which means I can enjoy them
when they are in glorious flower and
ignore them when they are looking
a bit yellow and defoliated. A great
climbing rose for cold-zone gardens is
'William Baffin'. This rose is incred-
ibly healthy and hardy with flowers
that are a show-stopper pink.

**Red Malabar Spinach
(*Basella rubra*)**
Every vegetable garden needs a
vine or two. Strictly speaking, most
indeterminate tomato plants are
vines (unlike the bushy determinate

tomatoes that set a single large
crop of fruit). Only once we have
accepted that fact will we ever give
them the tall, strong support they
need. The flimsy metal cones sold as
tomato cages in most garden centers
are laughably inadequate.

A much more unusual choice of
edible climber is Malabar spinach.
Not a true spinach at all, though
it can be enjoyed like spinach, this
tropical vine from India regrows
quickly so it can (and should) be
continually harvested. The dark
red stems and deep green leaves
look wonderful on a trellis or other
tall structure. Even if you prefer
ordinary spinach, most gardeners
can only grow spinach in the cooler
spring and autumn months. Because
of its tropical origins, Malabar spinach fills the summer gap, offering
spinachlike leaves all summer long.

Sweet Peas (*Lathyrus odoratus*)
Old-fashioned, scented sweet
peas are unfamiliar to many

Americans—you won't find sweet peas in supermarket bouquets, and they don't grow well in hot weather, which most North American gardens have for most of the summer. These flowers are obvious members of the pea family, but they are mildly poisonous. Do not confuse the seedpods with edible peas. They require support for their twining, curling vines and frequent harvesting to keep them from setting seed and ceasing flower production. If all this sounds far too difficult to manage, then all I can say is that once you have buried your nose in a handful of scented sweet peas you will forever add at least one packet—and maybe a few more—to your annual seed order.

Though I only knew the flowers from reading British literature (sweet peas love the cool UK summers), I now count successfully growing sweet peas as one of the great achievements of my life. And perhaps even of my marriage—Jonathan made two sweet pea "tunnels" for me in our former vegetable garden. Using rebar and wire mesh, he created an arched trellis of sorts that connected one raised bed to another, allowing garden visitors to walk through a tunnel of sweet pea flowers. A sweet pea tunnel may require a bit of work and preparation, but it is surely one of the wonders of our world.

Trumpet Honeysuckle (*Lonicera sempervirens*)

Honeysuckle is both the stuff of sweet childhood memories (who hasn't plucked a trumpet blossom and sipped nectar like a honeybee?) and the stuff of more grown-up nightmares. Imported honeysuckles like Japanese honeysuckle (*Lonicera japonica*) have, in many parts of North America, spread aggressively across natural areas, suppressing the growth of native plants.

Fortunately, conscientious gardeners can choose other honeysuckle varieties that make better neighbors in an American garden. Varieties of trumpet or coral honeysuckle (*Lonicera sempervirens*) are beautiful growing up garden structures or left to romp across the ground as ground cover. Although they do not have the enticing scent of a Japanese honeysuckle, their color and form are striking. Best of all, they are a guilt-free vine.

Maypop or Purple Passionflower (*Passiflora incarnata* and Hybrids)
My first encounter with the passionflower vine that is native across the southeastern United States came soon after our move to Florida, when I spotted it climbing a rustic wooden fence around a local butterfly garden. I could hardly believe the large, frilly, exuberant flowers were real. Until then, I had not known that a butterfly-attracting, fruit-producing, American native vine could be such a visual stunner.

A LAYERED GARDEN

There is a phenomenon in the world of gardening known as the June gap, and gardeners—like riders of the London Underground—would be well-advised to "mind the gap." No matter when exactly it arrives (in my own garden it usually occurs somewhere around mid- to late May) it can feel as if the garden is taking a deep breath after the flurry of spring blossom. The late-spring gap is the moment between daffodil and honeysuckle. It is the silence between tulip and rose. It is the quiet, green pause between the song of cherry blossom and the tune of trumpeting lilies. I have always been aware of this pause between the flowers of spring and the flowers of summer, but I was never more aware than last year when I decided to host a big, ambitious garden party in the very middle of May.

As is often the case when scheduling, I landed on this date after much discussion and reflection and staring at the calendar. I thought about Mother's Day. I thought about the weather (in my garden spring can veer cold but early summer can veer hot). I considered the date of our daughter's graduation. Simply put, I considered every last thing except this: what would be in flower? For garden parties are not really garden parties without something in flower. That year, we had an especially drawn out and chilly spring. Two weeks before the party I panic-purchased two large patio heaters. Now it was the first of May, and I could see that my only hope for garden glory lay in the lingering spring flowers: white dogwood blossom, the summer snowflake bulbs (properly called *Leucojum*), and the later flowering 'White Triumphator' tulips. I began to pray, "Dear God, let the white flowers of late spring hang on because the summer flowers are still weeks away!" While I hoped it would warm up enough for an evening party to feel enjoyable, I also hoped it wouldn't warm up too much, too soon, causing my tall white tulips to drop their petal skirts before party day.

Who plans a garden party right smack in the middle of the dreaded *gap*? This gardener, apparently. Perhaps my error can be blamed on the fact that over the years of my gardening here at Maplehurst, all sorts of gaps have grown smaller and less noticeable. For instance, I used to have a great wide gap between the daffodils that grew unbothered by deer alongside our driveway and the tulips I planted in more protected places near the house. But this gap only existed because I mostly planted early-flowering yellow daffodils and late-flowering specialty tulips, the kind with doubled petals and fringed edges. Over the years, I have deliberately begun to plant both the earliest yellow daffodils, like 'February Gold' and 'Rijnveld's Early Sensation', which grow very true to their names, and the extremely late-flowering white poeticus daffodils like 'Pheasant's Eye' and 'Actaea'. At the same time, I make sure to choose tulips in single and double forms that bloom in early, mid-, and late spring. The same approach toward season extension can be applied to roses and iris and even magnolia trees.

I imagine planning and growing a garden is something like composing a symphony. There may be great swells of sound here and there, but I try to pay attention to the pauses in order to create a more complex and layered composition. There is the pause in flowering when a garden can look a bit dull and colorless. This is a gap felt in time. There is also a kind of gap we feel spatially when we see gaps in our planting beds themselves. When I first began to grow flowers, I was thrilled to watch bulbs I had planted in fall emerge in crayon colors in spring. I noted that my colorful tulips did not make a visual impression quite so beautiful as the displays in more professional gardens, but I assumed bare soil was a given in early spring. It took a comment from my friend Julie Witmer before

I understood what my eyes had been telling me all along: colorful tulips are not set off to perfection by a bed of boring, brown mulch. My tulips were always growing out of bare beds covered in brown. My garden was missing some key layers.

Since then, I've begun to fill in my beds with more perennials, so my tulips now emerge more regularly in the company of sedums just beginning to expose the green rosettes of their early growth. I love to plant crocus and scilla bulbs and sweet alyssum in those same beds for very early color. And I am determined one day to mimic the effect I have admired at Chanticleer Garden outside Philadelphia by sowing lettuce seed around my tulips. The result is practical *and* beautiful. This kind of layering is important on the macro as well as micro level. If you take the time to really study a natural woodland landscape, you will see layers that shift from sky to the canopy of tall trees, to the dappled sunlight shining on smaller understory trees, before falling on shrubs, then herbaceous perennials, and all the way down to ground cover plants. Though garden design is inherently contrived—a kind of beautiful artifice—nature has a wisdom gardeners do well to heed. Earth and sky long for a visual connection through plants. Even soil wants to be covered. We can use chipped, brown bark mulches, but wouldn't a living, green mulch from ground cover plants look more beautiful?

One final garden layer revealed itself at my May garden party: light. The first flowers to fade each day in our gardens are those darker colored ones that quickly dissolve into the oncoming shadows of evening. As the sun lowers itself, our colorful garden flowers disappear from sight, one after the other, until all we have left is palest pink, then palest yellow, and finally only white. White flowers glow like torches in the evening. They reflect back to us even the little light that the moon and stars give. Last May, in the darkness after the party ended, I could no longer see the roses I had hastily bought and planted in containers. I could not see the lavender topiaries I had been thrilled to find at a big-box store. But my eyes were still caught on every one of the 'White Triumphator' tulips. All on their own, they had shown up for party day with bells on. The evening was fully dark, and yet there they were, glowing brightly with the last of the candles. It seemed right and good that they were the final garden party guests to say goodnight.

GROUND-HUGGERS

Ground-covering plants can be afterthoughts in our garden design, but it is important to get this layer right if only to save ourselves quite a bit of backbreaking labor down the line. If we gardeners don't cover our soil, the weeds will happily do the job for us. What's more, ground cover plants can enhance the beauty of every other plant in our garden, which means that the smallest plants have the potential to contribute the most.

Ground cover is not really a type of plant. Rather, it is how we use the plant that gives it this name. The catmint (Nepeta) I use as a ground cover in my flower garden might be much too large and unwieldy to serve that role in your own garden, while something quite large like a Miscanthus ornamental grass might cover the ground effectively if planted en masse on a large slope.

1. **Carex:** There are many types of sedges for different growing conditions. I love Pennsylvania sedge (*Carex pensylvanica*) for a soft, flowing green beneath shade trees and shrubs.

2. **Catmint (*Nepeta*):** The plant I am asked about most often in my own garden is *Nepeta racemosa* 'Walker's Low'. The purple wand-like flowers are often confused with lavender, but catmint, unlike Mediterranean lavender, thrives in my heavy, wet soil.

3. **Green and gold (*Chrysogonum virginianum*):** This North American native won the award for longest blooming in my garden last year with its bright yellow, daisylike flowers.

4. **Stonecrop (*Sedum* and hybrid crosses such as *Hylotelephium telephium* 'Autumn Joy'):** Some

upright sedums can reach three feet tall, but I like to think of them as ground cover partners. For instance, a bed of spring tulips will be set off to perfection by the emerging rosettes of 'Autumn Joy'. By the time the sedum have grown tall, the tulip leaves have died back.

5. Lilyturf (*Liriope muscari*): This clumping—not spreading—lilyturf looks a bit like an ornamental grass but handles shade with aplomb. I grow both variegated and deep green varieties and always appreciate their late-summer purple flowers.

6. Creeping thyme (*Thymus praecox*): An aromatic option for those gardening in drier climates or for those with well-drained rock gardens or stone patios where this low-growing thyme can be left to spread.

7. Sweet alyssum (*Lobularia maritima*): I always start a tray of these annuals from seed each winter. Alyssum makes a beautiful blooming carpet to fill in bare patches in my flower garden. As well, it makes a great "filler and spiller" for containers.

8. Barrenwort (*Epimedium*): This perennial thrives in dry shade on more acidic soils. The heart-shaped leaves are the real stunner, but the delicate flowers are a definite bonus.

9. Spotted dead nettle (*Lamium maculatum*): A thousand times more beautiful than their name, spotted dead nettles are perennial shade-lovers with pink, purple, or white flowers. Some varieties have beautifully variegated foliage. If hot weather singes your *lamium*, simply cut the affected leaves back to stimulate fresh growth.

10. Black chokeberry (*Aronia melanocarpa*): Low-growing varieties of this North American native shrub make a beautiful, bird-friendly ground cover.

11. **Ferns:** A mass of ferns can be one of the most beautiful and effective ground covers beneath trees. Seek out varieties suitable for your growing conditions and perhaps even native to your local woodlands.

12. **Sweet woodruff (*Galium odoratum*):** This special plant always makes me think of fairies. It's magical with its soft green leaves and starry white flowers. It is reputed to be both deer- and rabbit-proof, which seems likely given how long it has persisted beneath an old maple on the edge of my garden.

WHOLE GARDENS FOR WHOLE GARDENERS

In my own country, we call the land around a house the "yard." We have back-yards and front yards. We even have side yards. We also have gardens, but when we use that word we typically mean the area of tilled ground or the collection of raised beds somewhere within the yard where we grow our tomatoes. In my country, it is quite possible to hear someone say that they have no garden when they do, in fact, have a quarter acre or more of land with foundation borders around their home, various shrubs, and perhaps even a few trees. But all this does not, in my country, add up to a garden.

In some other English-speaking countries I could name—countries with long histories of ornamental gardening—the land around a house is called the "garden." It is always called the garden, even when it is a neglected garden. It is called a garden even if only trees or only shrubs or only lawn grows there. It is called the garden even if no gardener is growing tomatoes or indeed any food at all. The word *garden* simply refers to a private or enclosed parcel of land. It may be bursting with green and colorful life, or the name may only describe its potential, but the assumption is that a house with land around it is a house sitting in a garden.

This may represent only a quirk of the English language. It may be nothing more than one of those funny anecdotes we tell one another when we are laughing at the strangeness of our native tongue. But I wonder if we should give our language more credit than that. I wonder if we should reckon with the power it does in fact wield in our lives. What would change if I and my neighbors began referring to the ground around our homes as gardens? Would we see a potential we had not noticed before? Would we call ourselves gardeners without worrying so much about whether we have green thumbs or not? Would we, perhaps, make room for our tomatoes *and* a few more ornamental plants?

It makes sense to me that we call our land the yard because we are such practical, utilitarian people, as a rule. Perhaps it is a legacy of our national heritage as immigrant farmers, yet few of us today use our yards for anything like practical agriculture. Beyond serving as a place for kicking the soccer ball or turning cartwheels, ordinary grass lawns don't serve much practical purpose at all. Some might call them beautiful, and they do feel wonderful under bare feet, but their beauty is one-dimensional rather than deep and whole. Most lawn grasses grow only very shallow roots, which do little to help aerate soil to any significant depth. The clovers that fix nitrogen and feed soil, along with the dandelions that nourish important pollinators, are generally not invited to our American lawn parties despite how much they have to offer.

Perhaps we would be more accurate to say that a perfect green lawn is a pretty thing while reserving our use of the word *beautiful* for those garden elements that are rooted, connected, and whole. In the vegetable garden, we might admire the pretty, pale yellow of a summer squash and the pretty, round leaves of nasturtium flowers, but when we understand that nasturtiums help limit the number of squash bugs in our gardens, then we might rightly call a bed of intermingled squash and nasturtiums *beautiful*. It isn't only the colors and flavors that are beautiful—it is the interconnected, mutually beneficial partnership. It is the beauty of a rooted, connected whole.

How do we grow whole gardens? I think we begin by turning our gaze inward and inspecting our own places of hunger and lack. We ask ourselves not what

others expect of us, but what we truly love. Is it the image of a tire swing dangling beneath a giant shade tree? Is it the bouquet of cheerful sunflowers that tempts us every week at the farmers' market? Is it birdsong? A memory of making mud pies? The dream of picking your own plums? Perhaps our places cannot fulfill every dream, but that mud pie memory might fuel a grown-up obsession with potted petunias on a city balcony. Stranger things have happened, and I can personally draw a line connecting scented stargazer lilies at a South Side Chicago farmers' market to balcony petunias with a view of downtown to a farmhouse where lilies grow in perfumed abundance. Life begets life.

I am more and more convinced there are two kinds of people: professional gardeners and all the rest of us regular gardeners. Choose the rooted basil and parsley from the supermarket instead of the snipped herbs in a plastic clamshell, remember to keep them watered near your kitchen window, and—just like that—you are gardening. Anything could be next, even a legacy shade tree that will become a nursery for butterflies, a perch for songbirds, and a pantry for squirrels. Your garden might be whole and complete with herbs on the windowsill and a native shade tree in the garden. Your garden might be whole and complete with a row of sunflowers, half for you to cut and half left to feed the birds. Your garden will be whole when you stop worrying what the neighbors think or whether you will be outed as a gardening fraud and start listening to your heart—your verdant heart—in order to tend the many and various seeds of life.

PART FOUR

GARDENS GROW HOPE

April, dressed in all his trim,
Hath put a spirit of youth in every thing.

WILLIAM SHAKESPEARE, "SONNET XCVIII"

THE ART OF WILDNESS

Once upon a time, gardens were the opposite of wild places. In an age when wild landscapes with their wild weather and wild animals could kill you, gardens were sanctuaries. They were safe because they were enclosed. They were beautiful because they were artfully made. They were peaceful because within them grew plants for medicine and plants to delight the senses. In myths, the sea is chaos. In fairy tales, the forest is the home of evil. In all our stories, gardens are paradise. But while the tales and stories and their age-old archetypes remain, the earth itself has changed irrevocably: no part of the sea is too remote for our plastic garbage, forests are clear-cut then "managed" for optimum productivity, and gardens require "maintenance" with machines and chemicals. Where, then, is our sanctuary? Where can we go to find peace? Is there any place left that is safe from our insatiable human greed? I believe the garden can still be this place, if we are willing to make room in our gardens for wildness.

Though wild places do still exist, for most North American gardeners, wildness is limited to the raccoon who disturbs the trash bin at night and deer who wander through our neighborhoods eating hostas and rosebushes. Wildness is a nuisance. Why would we ever want more of it? One answer is buried deep in our brains. For most of human history, and certainly prehistory, we have lived in a visual world of curves, soft edges, and meandering lines. Our brains developed in savannas, not indoor shopping malls or office blocks. Yet today, we primarily live in a world of hard edges and straight lines. We are surrounded by concrete, asphalt, steel, and vinyl. Real prairies where a sea of grass moves with the wind are almost entirely a thing of the past. Real forests are something we must journey to see during one vacation week a year or one weekend hike a month. The natural places of the earth have receded to the far edges of our daily, lived experience. No wonder our brains are overstimulated. No wonder our nervous systems are exhausted. No wonder our mental health suffers. And while these are complex issues with complex causes, one solution is simple: we can grow gardens that in some small way allow our bodies and our brains to return to nature.

Of course, gardens are, by definition, places cared for by a gardener, and so in some sense, they will always stand in opposition to wildness. And yet, savvy gardeners can design and care for places in ways that evoke natural landscapes and invite the abundant wildlife of bees and birds and butterflies. It is a very fine line that might actually involve drawing a few lines with a mower. Grass left to grow tall might look unkempt, but mow a meandering path through its middle, and you immediately create a visual meadow and a strong sense of place, not to mention a lovely invitation to stroll. A wildflower patch might look more like a weed patch (and might even *be* a weed patch!), but give it a sharp, clean edge with a mower or a spade, and the weed patch will automatically look intentional. One of my favorite small tricks is to mow a neat circle around the trunks of my apple trees. The result requires less maintenance—I no longer need to use a weed trimmer right up to the bark of my tree—and achieves a slightly wild orchard look as clover and dandelions bloom their weedy little heads off beneath the bobbing apples. Sometimes less is more in every way.

But what if your garden is a small one? A garden where orchards and meadows would never fit? A small garden is an opportunity to forgo lawn altogether in favor of beds and borders or to grow a "bee lawn." Seed mixes are now available for "lawns" that require little mowing and are full of flowering clovers and thymes to feed pollinators. A small plot is also a wonderful place for a cottage-style

garden where flowers and herbs and fruits and vegetables grow cheek by jowl and cabbages are as pretty as roses. The effect might not be quite natural, but it is certainly a bit wild, and it is still capable of inviting in the kind of wildlife Beatrix Potter celebrated in her children's books. And whether your garden is large or small, everyone has room for the wildest addition of all: water. Dig a pond and grow lilies or half-bury a small plastic tub and grow a single lily—either way, you will discover that the most effective way to add more wildlife to your gardens is by making room for water. Add a pond, and they will come. Birds will come, toads will come, dragonflies will come, life will come. Few activities could be more soothing and more healing for our psyches than losing ourselves for a while in the iridescent blue wings of a water-skimming dragonfly.

Because the world has changed (or rather, because *we* have changed the world), our culture of gardening must change. Even our definition of *sanctuary* must shift. The word *sanctuary* comes from a Latin word for a container used to keep holy objects or cherished things, even cherished people. Today, then, our gardens cannot function as true sanctuaries if we tend them in ways that keep life *out*. If we cherish birds and bees and butterflies—and children!—as well as green leaves and flowers and waving grasses, then our gardens should be containers for all these. In so many ways the world we have made has become hostile to life. When we garden, we have the opportunity to create places where life is nurtured. If we allow our gardens to become a little messier, a little wilder, then paradoxically we'll find it that much easier to discover what the poet Wendell Berry has called the "peace of wild things."[3] And where there is peace, there is hope.

FULLY ALIVE LAWNS

Some ecologically minded gardeners have taken to calling our American grass lawns—often grown with chemical fertilizers, pesticides, gas-fueled machines, and copious amounts of irrigation—"deadscapes" rather than landscapes. If you want to bring more life to your lawn, here are only a few of the many enticing possibilities.

"Bee lawn" seed mixes: More and more pollinator-friendly specialty seed mixes are becoming available. Often called "bee lawns" or "pollinator lawns," they make use of low-growing, flowering plants like clover and thyme that rarely need mowing.

Carex: There are sedges for just about every garden. While these grasslike plants can't handle as much foot traffic as ordinary turf grasses, they can provide a beautiful, soft expanse of green that only needs to be trimmed a bit in spring.

Wild strawberries (*Fragaria virginiana*): Edible lawn, anyone? With white flowers in spring and red foliage in fall, wild strawberries make an excellent ground cover plant or lawn alternative, even in light shade, as well as offer up sweet and tasty berries.

Lawn grass with flowering clover: If clover is already "invading" your lawn, then encourage it to spread by neglecting to mow while it is in flower. White clover often blooms in May, which has led to a popular campaign called "no-mow May."

Moss: If you already have moss growing in your lawn, that's a good sign the site is less than suitable for grasses. Embrace the gift you've been given by encouraging it to spread. Pull out turf grass and weeds and keep your moss clear of twigs and other debris. If you want to purchase moss, look for sustainable sources like Mountain Moss Enterprises, which rescues moss from places slated for development.

THE GENEROUS GARDEN

I am convinced the reason more of my friends and neighbors don't garden is because we all begin gardening by attempting the most difficult kinds of gardening. We start out, for the most part, either with houseplants or vegetables. Indoor container gardening is difficult because the gardener must meet every single one of her plant's needs. Nature can offer no help inside the four walls of our homes. And vegetable gardening is a great deal of work because it is a form of productive gardening. Most food crops must continually be sown and harvested and protected from pests and diseases and then sown again. It is more like farming than other kinds of gardening, and we all know that farming is very hard work. No wonder so many of us declare our thumbs black and call it a day, leaving our raised beds to become graveyards for weeds. Of course, those who persevere reap the sweet rewards of oxygenated indoor air or a bounty of tomatoes. It is more than worthwhile learning how to tend houseplants and how to garden productively for homegrown harvests. But if your experience with gardening has largely been one of failure and disappointment, I suggest beginning again and beginning again with more generous, hospitable garden plants. I recommend edible perennials like thornless blackberries, asparagus, and even ostrich ferns.

If that last suggestion surprises you, it is likely because we tend not to let our thoughts wander far from the categories and labels and boxes that are handed down to us. We know about annuals that do not return and perennials that do. We know about ornamental plants for making gardens beautiful and edible plants for cooking and eating. But we tend to forget that ostrich ferns are beautiful ornamental landscape plants that give delicious fiddleheads for eating in spring. And what about rhubarb? Bright stems, large leaves, perennial, *and* delicious stewed with strawberries. These two could not be more different from vining, indeterminate tomatoes. Though most gardeners find them well worth the effort, they are not exactly plants for Gardening 101. First, seed must be sown indoors. Even if we buy our tomatoes already started, we must keep an eye on the weather and soil temperature, for tomatoes cannot abide even a bit of cold. If they do get off to a healthy start, we must tie them to supports, prune out excess stems, water and feed them, and harvest as they ripen, while continuing to tie them in, water and feed, and prune out excess stems. Compare that with ostrich ferns, which only need their dead fronds cut away in late winter or early spring to better reveal the emerging (delicious!) smooth, jade-green fiddleheads of spring.

One of the best things I ever planted and then neglected here at Maplehurst was a variety of thornless blackberry called 'Chester'. I chose it because of my memories of picking backyard blackberries in Texas and because the name vaguely suggested some connection with my new Pennsylvania home in Chester County. To find the direct sun blackberries need, I planted my mail-order canes quite a distance from the house. Though I intended to take good care of my new blackberry patch, I have since found that distance from the house is directly correlated with distance from my thoughts, and thus my blackberries have been sadly neglected over the years. More often than not, I have failed to weed and mulch them, have forgotten to cut out the old canes that fruited the previous season, and have rarely, if ever, given them compost for food. And yet, after a slow start while they put their energy into growing roots rather than fruit, we have harvested enough berries every July for snacking and cobbler making. They have become the ultimate set-it-and-forget-it edible plants. I feel only slightly guilty about the fact that I never remember them until they are setting fruit. Because gardening can be such hard work, I take easy where I find it, and these blackberries have been surprisingly easy. If I gave them more, would I receive more in return? Undoubtedly. But I give almost nothing and still receive cobblers, so I'm not going to waste too much time worrying about this particular garden gift horse.

One of the best things I never planted, and definitely neglect, in my garden are the wineberries. Like a soft, sweet raspberry, wineberries grow wild in the shady, neglected edges of my garden and in many of the wild, untended areas of southeastern Pennsylvania. Also called wine raspberries or Japanese wineberries (*Rubus phoenicolasius*), these thorny, suckering shrubs are not native to North America but were introduced from Asia in the nineteenth century. They are considered invasive in my state because they can grow into such large, impenetrable mats that they prohibit native berries from growing and can even keep native tree seedlings from emerging to renew our forests. The good news, however, is that one of the best ways to keep wineberry seeds from becoming new wineberry shrubs is by eating the berries. So, while one day I might grub out my shrubs to plant native woodland treasures, for now I do my part by picking bowlfuls of berries each July. And wild-grown fruits aren't only a Pennsylvania treat. New England has blueberries and the South has muscadine grapes. Many places have blackberries—some places even have a relative called dewberry—and many of us can forage for elderberries, mulberries, and chokeberries. Of course, the safest foraging is the foraging we do in our own backyards, and the easiest gardening we accomplish might simply occur when we let things go a bit wild and then watch to see what grows. Dandelion wine, anyone?

PLANTING FOR THE FUTURE

Asparagus (*Asparagus officinalis*)
A well-kept asparagus bed might give harvests for thirty springs, as long as the newly planted crowns are left unharvested for the first three growing seasons. The writer Barbara Kingsolver describes how she put in asparagus beds at every house she ever owned as an adult—and a few she only rented—"always leaving behind a vegetable legacy."[4]

Peonies (*Paeonia lactiflora*),
Daylilies (*Hemerocallis*),
Crinum Lilies (*Crinum*)
Herbaceous perennial peonies are among the longest-lived flowering garden plants. *Herbaceous* simply

means they die back to the ground in winter. *Perennial* means exactly what it sounds like: late-spring beauties that return year after year after year. And despite some commonly heard myths, peonies can be transplanted. August is a great time to do it as the plant has already begun to fade and wither. But take care not to plant them too deep since this can prevent flowering.

For those gardening in warmer zones without enough winter cold for peonies, **daylilies** are beautiful, rugged, and long-lived. **Crinum lilies** are another adaptable and enduring summer flower for warmer climates. The renowned Plant Delights Nursery catalog calls them "a horticultural IRA for your grandkids to remember you by."

Black Walnut Trees (*Juglans nigra*)
Too many old garden books had me convinced for a long time that the giant black walnut tree towering over our barn was a nuisance. Walnuts secrete a toxic chemical into the soil around their roots that prevents competing garden plants from growing. At least, that is what I've always read. But it turns out that many plants native to the same eastern American woodlands as the walnuts grow just fine planted in juglone-laced soil. It is primarily our imported, exotic plants that call it poison.

Native Americans used the bark and leaves medicinally. They valued walnuts in their diets, as did European colonists, who planted the majestic trees we often see today around old homesteads. I grieve to think that generations have failed to plant new walnut trees from fear of their "poison." Today, I have neighbors who gather the black walnuts from the old trees on their family vineyard in order to flavor an exquisite Spanish-style vermouth. My husband and I both love to sip a small glass of Casa Carmen vermouth in the shade beneath our lacy-leaved walnut tree. Someday, I will plant a young walnut—far from my vegetable garden—so future generations can know the same joy, and I hope you'll do the same. Just don't plant your tree too near your asparagus patch.

CHOOSE YOUR OWN ADVENTURE

A funny thing we humans like to do is discover some good path and promptly claim it as the only way, as if good were only good when it is also best. Of course, this isn't only a funny habit, it is actually quite a tragic propensity of ours. It diminishes an infinitude of goodness to a single narrow thread. In fact, it ascribes to goodness a quality that really belongs to its opposite. On the eve of World War II, the French philosopher Simone Weil wrote that despite evil's literary reputation for being "romantic" and "varied," real evil was actually "monotonous, barren, boring." Goodness, she insisted, was "always new, marvelous, intoxicating."[5] After the war, another philosopher, Hannah Arendt, would famously coin the phrase "the banality of evil" to describe the evil organized by Nazi bureaucrats. While the great English poet John Milton depicted evil as quite a seductive figure, and countless artists, writers, and even preachers have followed in his footsteps, Weil and Arendt stuck pins in that inflated view. Evil is boring, they said. Good is something else entirely.

If war is the right context for a close study of evil, a garden is just the right place for encountering goodness. This is not so surprising if we recall that the story of good and evil begins, for many, in a garden. While evil takes root in Eden because one rule is disobeyed, there is not one single way to do good in the garden, because goodness is so much more expansive than that. Too often, humans make everything a kind of war. In the world of gardening, this can look like heirlooms versus hybrids, native plants versus exotic imports, productive gardening versus ornamental. Good versus bad. Us against them. Everything only black or white. But though this is our regrettable human tendency, it is a tendency with no place in the glorious, fruitful riot of a garden.

In a garden, we are invited to choose our own good adventure. Perhaps we might walk the path of a seed saver. In the autumn, we head out with our little paper envelopes, our pencils for labeling, and we gather the seeds that our gardens have produced. Travel far enough down this road, taking care to gather seed only from those open-pollinated plants that have performed the best, and we can develop our own genetic seed strains exactly adapted to the conditions of our microclimates and our own very particular soil. But even this excellent way is not the only way nor the best way. We might choose instead to buy fresh seed each year from worthy heirloom seed producers like Seed Savers Exchange and others. If no one buys the seed and plants the seed from these specialty growers, then special varieties can be lost. Purchasing heirloom seeds, rather than saving them, is one more way to do good. Which way will you choose? Or, like a child reading every possible ending to a choose-your-own-adventure book, will you choose both?

When I lost my first large raised-bed vegetable garden to the rerouting of our driveway, I felt as if I had also lost my homesteading credentials. Who was I without cucumbers to ferment and tomatoes to stew and freeze? But I soon realized that without a vegetable garden of my own, I was free to support the efforts of so many other local growers. Instead of harvesting my own snap peas, I bought them from the Amish family at a nearby market. Without room to grow my own pumpkins and melons, I made a tour of local farmsteads looking for the best and the sweetest. Without my own strawberry bed, I made sure to visit the nearest U-pick farm on an early June morning. I want to live in a community with a thriving culture of food production, but as long as I had my own garden, I missed out on the opportunity to

support local growers with my grocery budget. It wasn't wrong to grow my own. It wasn't wrong to not grow my own. It was a good thing to grow my own food, and it is also a good thing to buy food others have grown locally. Which is best? Perhaps there is no best, only that which is best for us each year.

This choose-your-own-adventure approach to doing good in our gardens is especially helpful with the perennially thorny question of native plants. When something as important as supporting local ecosystems is at stake, gardeners can become understandably impassioned about "best" practices. We might wonder whether we are ever justified in giving space in our gardens to non-native plants. And what about so-called nativars, those hybrid varieties bred from native species that might not support wildlife as well as their native parents do? If setting a goal and pursuing it with perfectionistic zeal brings you joy, then making it your goal to grow a garden that supports the local ecosystem as much as possible is a worthy goal. One of my friends has chosen the adventure of growing a garden devoted almost entirely to our local bird populations. If there is a native plant that helps birds, then you can bet she grows it. The only thing she grows purely for herself each summer is a 'Brandywine' tomato. But another gardener might make it her goal to grow an ornamental garden that persuades her neighbors to grow native plants too. This gardener might include nativars amongst her native species to boost the visual appeal of the garden as a whole. In this way, she might encourage those skeptical of weedy-looking gardens to include native plants in their gardens. This, too, is a worthy adventure.

The good news about this expansive view of goodness is that it allows every kind of garden in every kind of place with every kind of gardener to be, in its own way, a very good garden. Goodness, it turns out, is like water: flowing, filling, moving, spreading. It takes the form of its vessel, it is different in every place, and yet it is always also itself. It is good. As I imagine a new productive garden for Maplehurst, I think of the particular good that seems right for me and for this place. I want to grow ground cherries again because they are difficult if not impossible to find at my local markets, and they make the most delicious and most beautiful jam. I may not, however, grow zucchini or summer squash or green beans. I might just let local growers take care of those tasks for me. I would like to grow my own asparagus, but I think I will plant a green variety and also buy a purple kind each spring at the local farm stand. More asparagus in April is surely a very good thing.

The labor of gardening is hard enough without placing additional burdens on our shoulders or on the shoulders of other would-be growers. The single-minded pursuit of best might be right for some gardeners, but thankfully there is so much good outside the narrow boundaries of best. Goodness isn't a trickle of water, and it isn't a narrow canal. It is more like a wild river, splashing and turning and pulling us all— different as we may be—along for the ride. There is an ancient psalm that speaks of a river "whose streams make glad the city of God" (Psalm 46:4). I love to imagine the goodness of a garden like a laughing river. This is work, yes, but it is also play.

GROUND CHERRY JAM

Ground cherries are not a familiar fruit to most Americans despite their origins in the great plains of the Midwest. They are easy to grow from seed, but I have never spotted them at a supermarket or even a farmers' market. I thought I discovered them in the wonderful catalog of heirloom vegetables from Seed Savers Exchange, but while reading Laura Ingalls Wilder books with my youngest child, I realized I must have

encountered at least the name *ground cherry* as a young girl. In The
Long Winter, *a book I once read and reread obsessively, Wilder writes
that "Ma's wild ground-cherry preserves shone golden in a glass bowl."* [6]

*The flavor of a ground cherry can only be described as unexpected,
like a cross between a tomato and a pineapple. Sweetened and
made into jam, it is their golden color that makes them unforgettable.
Ground cherries readily self-sow from fallen fruit, just like volunteer
tomatoes, so once you get a plant or two going in your garden,
there's a good chance you'll never have to suffer through a long
winter without their sunshine color. The following recipe needs
two days but does not require any additional pectin.*

1. Over medium-low heat, place
   5 pints *husked* (papery skin
   removed) ground cherries, 2 cups
   sugar, and 3 tablespoons fresh
   lemon juice in a heavy-bottomed
   pot. I like to use enameled cast
   iron. Five pints come to about 1
   pound, 9 ounces ground cherries.

2. Once the sugar has dissolved,
   remove from heat, pour into a
   bowl, and cover. Store overnight
   in the refrigerator.

3. The following day, pour the
   ground cherry mixture back into
   your heavy-bottomed pot and
   bring to a boil over medium-high
   heat. Boil for 8 to 12 minutes or
   until your jam has set.

4. Jam can be stored in the
   refrigerator for up to three
   months. It can also be poured
   into sterilized jars and canned in
   a water bath just as you would
   other preserves for shelf storage.

HOPE IS BROWN
THEN GREEN

Gardening becomes a life-giving practice because gardeners become so well acquainted with death. We pencil it into our planners and calendars, writing the words *killing freeze* followed by the date. We sort dead things into hopeful piles, turning them with garden forks to speed the process of decay. We even begin to look forward to death. When a deep freeze finally blackens my dahlia plants in early November, I always say the same thing: "Finally!" After months of beautiful flowers, I am eager to complete the task of digging up my tubers and storing them safely for spring. I am eager to perfect my staking techniques next year with what I learned from failure this year. I am ready to stop growing a few disappointing types and make space for enticing new varieties from the local dahlia breeder I met this year. Deathly cold is a necessary thing, a turn of the wheel, a movement toward renewal. The returning seasons prove to us that the death that follows harvest always brings us one step nearer to seedtime. And the death of a seed is always one vital step nearer to harvest. Seedtime and harvest: these two are a matched pair, but the ties that bind them are life *and* death.

I was not sad the day we tore out the vegetable garden we had made our first springtime at Maplehurst. I had sowed heirloom seeds in that garden for five years. My youngest child learned to walk in that garden wearing tiny pink rain boots and holding on to the edge of a raised bed. I picked weeds in that garden and watched my little niece feed them to the chickens with pride. But my friend Lisa-Jo—who had never tended the garden, only visited it a few times a year—was much more devastated. You see, she was a happy garden visitor, and I was a tired, even somewhat discouraged, garden maker. When she arrived for an overnight stay sometime in early fall, the sight of our white picket fence unfenced and piled in a heap nearly brought tears to her eyes. "How could you?" her gaze said. "*Why* would you?" I assured her we would plant another vegetable garden in a better place, but inside I was full of secret doubts. "Maybe a large vegetable garden is too much for me? Maybe I should content myself with food from the farm stand?"

I did content myself with farm-stand produce for a few years. But now I feel a hunger growing in me that ready-bought produce alone cannot satisfy. I want to choose particular heirloom varieties, like the 'Strela Green' lettuce the Seed Savers Exchange catalog tells me dates to the 1500s. I want to plunge my hands into newly raked soil that I have fed with homemade compost. I want to sketch a plan for crop rotation and consider where exactly the shade of tall sunflowers should fall. Those are experiences I used to enjoy, but I needed a break from them in order once again to find them pleasurable. Usually, a winter break is enough. I fly out of the starting gate so fast each spring that by the end of a long, hot summer, even cooler fall weather can't revive me. But a few months spent largely indoors, often with a book by the wood stove, allows hope to grow again, as if all my end-of-season exhaustion and disappointment becomes compost for next year. My dahlias may have underperformed because of drought, but *next year* I won't neglect to hand water during dry spells. My tomato may have succumbed to disease, but *next year* I'll remember to prune away the lower leaves. *Next year*, I will be a better gardener, and I will tend a better garden.

Winter is no gardener's favorite season, and most of us hope every year that spring will come early. Yet a long winter—perhaps even a years-long winter—can be a gift of rest. It might be exactly what's needed for our garden and our

own selves to erupt with an abundance of life we have never experienced before. Gardening builds up within a gardener a resistance to despair. Year after year, we move from death to life and back from death to life, so that death no longer has the same hold on us. I used to grieve the loss of our enormous maple trees like one who mourned without hope. Now I find that friends and neighbors and visitors grieve much more intensely than I do. Again and again I find myself reassuring others: "I know. It's hard to lose a tree, but the time had come. See how hollow it was, all the way through? We'll plant a new tree here. Before we know it, fresh green leaves will scrape blue sky again."

First, hope is brown. It is the felled tree, the maple leaves on a compost pile, the raised bed in which we buried bulbs. Only later is hope green. It is the rabbit-ear tops of daffodils, the impossibly small whip of a baby apple tree, the shocking wick of green when we scrape our fingernail against a woody shrub we were sure had finally fully died. Years of gardening have tempered my despair and buttressed my hope. Today, as I write these words, my garden looks far less beautiful than it has in previous years. This week we had one more hollow maple and an enormous diseased hemlock tree taken down. The gigantic fresh tree stumps left behind look like jagged scars in a churned-up sea of mud. I was only half joking when I told my husband it all looked like Mordor, that accursed, treeless landscape in J.R.R. Tolkien's Middle-earth. The new vegetable garden I have planned for the area in front of the recently relocated chicken coop currently consists of two raised-bed frames in a pile where they were tossed to make way for the removal of two dead antique cherry trees. The whole western side of Maplehurst is like one great swathe of destruction, and the view through my bedroom window as I type on this January day is a view of death.

Yet I have hope. This place, these gardening years, have given me a persistent, resilient hope. I still don't know if my fingers are green, but my heart is surely verdant. Tall trees grow from small seeds, and large vegetable gardens grow from a dream and some hard work, and where we've done it once, we can do it once more. Gardens will grow here. Hope is rooted here. My eyes see only brown, but my heart sees that brown is only one shade away from the brightest, freshest green.

A YEAR IN BULBS

Few things in the garden are as hopeful and energizing as a newly opened bulb in flower. While every climate and every garden are different, here are twelve bulbs and tubers that could give you an entire year of fresh, colorful hope.

January is for snowdrops (*Galanthus*).

February is for tommies (*Crocus tommasinianus*).

March is for the daffodil (*Narcissus*).

April is for the tulip (*Tulipa*).

May is for the drumbeat of ornamental onion (*Allium*).

June is for the first lilies (*Lilium*, Asiatic hybrids).

July is for the pineapple lily (*Eucomis*).

August in my garden is for gladioli or sword lilies (*Gladiolus*).

September is for dahlia (*Dahlia*).

October is for the autumn crocus (*Colchicum autumnale*).

November is for potting up an amaryllis indoors (*Hippeastrum*).

December is for paperwhites forced in glass jars (*Narcissus tazetta*).

HOPE IS GREEN
THEN RED

Seedtime is here. Though it is winter, though we have not yet even finished building and filling our raised beds, my new vegetable garden is beginning with bags of seed-starting soil, paper packets with pretty pictures, and fluorescent shop lights dangling from our root cellar's high ceiling. Yesterday, just as I began to gather my seed-starting supplies, my husband dropped a stack of mail on our kitchen table. On top was a padded yellow envelope from a friend in Texas. Kristen and I went to high school together, and though I don't remember whether we had much in common then, a few years ago we reconnected on Instagram and discovered a mutual passion for gardening. I tugged open the envelope with my finger, and though I knew what I would find, I didn't expect the overpowering scent. This ordinary yellow envelope had unleashed a fire that filled my nose with a familiar and particular sizzle. Kristen had sent me some of her very own homegrown dried bird peppers and bird pepper seeds.

Texas bird peppers are the only pepper native to North America. My mother-in-law calls them *pequin*. Kristen called them *chiltepin* in the note she included with her seeds, while Seed Savers Exchange sells them under the name McMahon's Texas Bird Pepper. The Aztecs called the pepper *chilli*, and the tiny heat-filled globes are still commonly known as *chili pequin*. When my mother-in-law left her longtime San Antonio home last year to live with us here at Maplehurst, she brought a few favorite pieces of furniture, Sadie her cockapoo dog, and a dozen or so pequin pepper seeds wrapped in a paper towel. I knew the seeds were the most important possession, with the possible exception of sweet Sadie, because, after all, how many times had I heard her tell us how her own father had kept red-hot pequins in the breast pocket of the formal suits he wore daily? Where other elegant men of his generation kept handkerchiefs or rosebuds, Rodolfo nurtured his northern Mexican roots with regular bites of the pequin peppers he ate like candy mints. The seeds my mother-in-law carried with her, the seeds she entrusted into my care, were like potent little memories and had actually grown from plants descended from those Rodolfo and his wife, Josefina, had tended themselves.

If asked, I might have said that my mother-in-law's seeds were the first bird pepper seeds to travel the San Antonio–to–Philadelphia route. I had certainly never encountered bird peppers on local farm stands. They are not winter hardy in my zone 6 garden and do not grow wild this far north. I might have remained ignorant of the bird pepper's story if failure hadn't sent me hunting, desperately, for more seeds. Last winter, when I started seeds for miniature bell peppers (which do well in a shorter growing season) and jalapeño peppers (which my husband likes to eat each night with dinner), I also started a small tray of the family peppers. Perhaps distracted by the needs of other seedlings, I allowed the potting soil to dry out. Or maybe the seeds had not been viable. Perhaps germination rates for pequins are always low. All I know for certain is that my mother-in-law had no fresh, homegrown bird peppers for what could be the first time in her life. I felt the failure keenly but tried to shrug it off. There are, after all, no guarantees in gardening.

In a garden, our perspective is always swinging like a pendulum between the vitality of tiny things—seeds, ladybugs, dewdrops—and the sheer abundance of seasons that turn quickly into years and on into generations. It is a harvest

of time and story too immense for any single one of us to gather, and yet we are a necessary part of it. Seed by seed. Memory after memory. My failure with those pepper seeds finally germinated something new when my gaze landed on a picture of McMahon's Texas Bird Peppers in the Seed Savers Exchange catalog. I had never heard that particular name before—McMahon. Could these be our family peppers? Indeed, they could be. They were. But more than a familiar description—tiny red peppers looking something like cranberries—the catalog gave me a story I never knew. Around the year 1812, a certain Captain Samuel Brown was stationed in San Antonio, a city that was then central to the conflict between Spain and a Mexico set on independence. Brown corresponded with the author of the American Declaration of Independence. He sent pepper seeds to Monticello, explaining to Thomas Jefferson that the dried peppers "were as essential to my health as salt itself." Jefferson grew the seeds and sent some to Philadelphia nurseryman Bernard McMahon, who sold the bird pepper as an ornamental plant. Pennsylvania food historian William Woys Weaver claims that "old Philadelphians used the potted peppers as a winter table ornament or as window sill plants. The peppers themselves were used to make pepper vinegar, pepper sauce, or pickles."[7]

The plant Jefferson called *Capsicum Techas*, the plant whose fruit is so beloved by birds because they are not bothered by the capsaicin that gives peppers their spice, the plant officially labeled *Capsicum annuum* var. *glabriusculum*, is a well-traveled pepper. Ours were not the first to make the journey. My friend Kristen's seeds will likely not be the last. But until I found the bigger story, I knew only our own small story of loss. The tiny seeds in their folded paper towel were family heirlooms, and I had let them die. I had ended a story we wanted to go on writing and telling and enjoying. I thought I was the central character in this tale, but I learned that I was only one of a large cast of gardeners, from old San Antonio to the garden at Monticello. My failure remains, but it was not a story-ending failure. The story will go on, and I like to think that my children will taste their first bird peppers this summer and my grandchildren will one day know the taste. Or if not the taste, in the event that they have inherited my own sensitive palate, I hope they become familiar with the sight of green hope slowly turning red on the kitchen windowsill of an old Pennsylvania farmhouse. "Here are your roots," I will say. "They are miles and years and generations long. Aren't they beautiful?"

EPILOGUE

Hope in an Age of Climate Chaos

Т his book began with ancient words that might have seemed like a simple statement of fact to a previous generation: "While the earth remains, seedtime and harvest, cold and heat, summer and winter, day and night, shall not cease" (Genesis 8:22 ESV). Today, they read like a promise. But will the promise be kept, or will it be broken? Gardeners pay attention to weather like no one else, and I am far from the only gardener who feels winter slipping away from her garden like so much January rain. Just this week, I read about a famous gardener in Connecticut who has seen his garden shift from growing zone 4 to growing zone 6 over the forty years of his tenancy there. He misses the legendary New England cold, but he is glad he can now grow the rare American native tree *Franklinia alatamaha*. It was narrowly saved from extinction in the late 1700s by Philadelphia plant collectors John and William Bartram.[8] I have only gardened a single decade at Maplehurst, but the average date of the first freeze has easily shifted two weeks later in this mere handful of years. Today, as I write, it is nearly February, and we have not seen even a dusting of snow.

Every leaf-scar is a bud expecting a future.

GILLIAN CLARKE, "THE YEAR'S MIDNIGHT"

Many of us have our stories to tell of unprecedented weather. We are gardening through atmospheric rivers of winter rain in California, withstanding extraordinary heat and drought in the English countryside, and, like my husband's colleague in Texas, learning how to insulate our aboveground water wells against the kind of arctic air that has never in our memory been unleashed so far south. Still, it's the scientists and data analysts who show us that what we sense and what we suspect can be tallied up in facts and numbers: oceans are warmer, glaciers are receding, storms are stronger, wildfire season is longer, and each summer is hotter than the last. How do we make gardens in the midst of climate chaos? How do we cultivate hope in an age of such uncertainty?

In the ancient wisdom text of Ecclesiastes, I find words that once communicated tedium. Today, they read to me like a comforting lullaby: "Generations come and generations go, but the earth remains forever. The sun rises and the sun sets, and hurries back to where it rises. The wind blows to the south and turns to the north; round and round it goes, ever returning on its course" (Ecclesiastes 1:4-6). For this writer, there is nothing new, all is the same, and it is "wearisome" (Ecclesiastes 1:8). But for me, the idea of an earth that never alters, in season and out, seems not wearisome but precious. That world would be solid ground under my feet. It would be a world in which winter visits my garden as it has always visited my garden. A world in which cool summer nights are, if not a guarantee, at least a regular possibility. Though I want to believe that the earth will not only remain but remain as I have known and loved it, I fear that in some sense it has tilted irrevocably on its axis and that nothing will ever be the same again.

On warm winter days, I find comfort in strange places: a novel about the fall of Constantinople, a philosopher's reflections on evil in 1943, my son's history homework on the black plague. These things remind me that so many different generations living in so many different places have been confronted with the end of the world as they've known it. My history-loving son and I listen to a podcast about the decline of the ancient Sumerian civilization, a culture that for thousands of years seemed invincible and inevitable, and I realize that almost since the dawn of recorded human history, the familiar, known world has been ending. Some might say that it is *really* ending this time. They may be right. Others might say that the loss of ice and snow does not matter so much (though I do not think these are the ones who live near rising seas). Yet it helps me to remember that my sense of helplessness and my grief for a familiar world forever changed are normal responses to an experience we humans have always known.

Making gardens in capricious and unpredictable climates is a challenge. Cultivating a hopeful posture toward the future isn't easy. Throwing our rusty old tomato cages in a pile and walking away is easy. Nostalgia for the past is easy. Even grief, in a way, is easy. But hope? Hope is a choice. Hope is a muscle. Hope is an action. Hope is a seed. Despite my fears and my uncertainties, I choose to root myself more deeply in my garden with each passing year, because the garden, while it is in some ways the source of my anxiety, is also the ground of my hope. Seeds break and die and are reborn. Even mild winters usher in spring. Nature is resilient. Polluted rivers have been healed, panda bears saved from extinction, and babies are still being born. Those babies will need gardens in which they can learn to walk. We must still give them raised beds for support and pretty flowers to pick for a parent. We must go on placing rain boots on their impossibly small feet. The daughter of mine who learned to use a watering can in a community garden in South Side Chicago is now all grown up and helping a nonprofit plant seeds of mercy and hope in Philadelphia. Acorns become oak trees even during our lifetimes. Generations come and generations go, and those who live as wise gardeners—in every sense—will sow gardens and harvest the fruit. They will have a hope. They will have a future.

When the larger picture becomes too much for me to comprehend, I return to the ordinary, small scale of my daily life. That is where all real change begins, after all. The seasons may feel out of tune, but gardens go on making beautiful music. Our weather is so mild I might step away from this computer and go in search of the hellebore planted beneath the old magnolia tree. They could be flowering. If the temperatures continue mild in February, I will go out and gather branches of forsythia and cherry to bring inside and force into early bloom. In March, if snow does not come, my husband and I will get a head start building the new raised beds. There are cool spring crops like radish, lettuce, and snap pea to sow. When rain falls, or if the weather turns cold, I will bury my nose in the leaves of the tomato seedlings down under grow lights in the basement. They smell exactly like red, ripe summer. Caring for my garden, I cease to be merely a thinking head full of worry. My head, heart, and body are reconciled again. Ready to dream and work again. Ready to watch my garden grow like a living miracle again. After all, it isn't certainty or guarantees that make the ground beneath our feet firm. It is love.

NOTES

1   Henry Mitchell, *The Essential Earthman: Henry Mitchell on Gardening* (Bloomington: Indiana University Press, 2008), 54.

2   Ken Druse, *The New Shade Garden: Creating a Lush Oasis in the Age of Climate Change* (New York: Stewart, Tabori & Chang, 2015), 149.

3   Wendell Berry, "The Peace of Wild Things," in *The Peace of Wild Things and Other Poems* (New York: Penguin, 2018), 25.

4   Barbara Kingsolver, *Animal, Vegetable, Miracle: A Year of Food Life* (New York: Harper Collins, 2007), 28.

5   Simone Weil, *Gravity and Grace*, trans. Arthur Wills (Lincoln: University of Nebraska Press, 1997), 120.

6   Laura Ingalls Wilder, *The Long Winter* (New York: Harper Trophy, 1971), 132.

7   William Woys Weaver, *Heirloom Vegetable Gardening: A Master Gardener's Guide to Planting, Seed Saving, and Cultural History* (Minneapolis: Voyageur Press, 2018), 311.

8   Lise Funderburg, "English Exuberance," *Garden Design*, Winter 2018, 49.

PLANT SOURCES

p. 2-3: *Rosa* 'Albertine'

p. 4: *Rosa* 'Lady of Shalott'

p. 7: *Rosa* 'Tottering-by-Gently'

p. 8: Against barn: 'Karl Foerster' feather reed grass; in bucket: zigzag goldenrod *Solidago flexicaulis*; in foreground pots: *Hydrangea paniculata* 'Bobo'

p. 11: Feather reed grass 'Karl Foerster'; *Rudbeckia* 'Goldsturm'

p. 12: *Verbena bonariensis*

p. 15: Zinnia 'Queen Lime Red'

p. 16: *Orlaya*

p. 19: *Echinops sphaerocephalus*

p. 20-21: Forget-me-not *Myosotis sylvatica*

p. 24-25: *Rosa* 'Music Box'

p. 28: *Rosa* 'Lady of Shalott'

p. 30: in containers: various hostas, *Plectranthus* 'Mona Lavender', Boston fern, and purple fountain grass; in bucket: *Veronica longifolia*

p. 32-33: *Hemerocallis* 'American Revolution' (daylily)

p. 39: *Liriodendron tulipifera* (tulip poplar tree)

p. 40: *Ilex verticillata* 'Winter Gold' (winterberry)

p. 42: Top: Japanese anemone 'Honorine Jobert'; bottom: varieties of *Helleborus*

p. 44: Prairie dropseed grass *Sporobolus heterolepis*

p. 47: 'Karl Foerster' feather reed grass; *Rudbeckia* 'Goldsturm'

p. 48: Northern sea oats *Chasmanthium latifolium*; *Verbena bonariensis*

p. 51: *Pennisetum alopecuroides* 'Hameln' (fountain grass); zigzag goldenrod *Solidago flexicaulis*

p. 52: 'Karl Foerster' feather reed grass

p. 54: Foreground to background: Bronze fennel, lacinato kale (also called Tuscan kale), flowering tobacco *Nicotiana sylvestris*

p. 57: 'Dara' chocolate lace flower

p. 58: Queen Anne's lace (wild carrot)

p. 60: Inch plant *Tradescantia zebrina*

p. 62-63: *Verbena bonariensis*

p. 68: fruit from 'Chicago Hardy' fig tree

p. 73: Dahlia 'Sincerity'

p. 74: Bronze fennel

p. 76: Top and bottom right: *Phlox paniculata* 'Jeana'; bottom left: Queen Anne's lace

p. 92: Top left: alpine strawberry 'Mignonette'; top right: Swiss chard 'Bright Lights'; bottom: lacinato kale (Tuscan kale)

p. 97: *Tagetes patula* 'Frances's Choice' (marigold)

p. 98: *Gladiolus callianthus* 'Murielae' (or Abyssinian Gladiolus)

p. 100: *Gaura* 'Whirling Butterflies'

p. 102-103: American elderberry *Sambucus canadensis*

p. 104: Queen Anne's lace, *Phlox paniculata* 'Jeana', *Lilium* 'Scheherazade'

p. 106-107: 'Dara' chocolate lace flower, anise hyssop

p. 110: Anise hyssop

p. 112: Zigzag goldenrod *Solidago flexicaulis*

p. 115: Pale Purple Coneflower *Echinacea pallida*

p. 116: *Echinops sphaerocephalus*

p. 118: top: *Helianthus annuus* 'Moonshadow' (sunflower); bottom left and right: *Helianthus annuus* 'Sunfinity' (sunflower)

p. 120: *Wisteria frutescens* 'Nivea' (American wisteria)

p. 122-123: left: *Rosa* 'Zéphirine Drouhin'; right: *Rosa* 'Albertine'

p. 126: *Rosa* 'Zéphirine Drouhin'

p. 129: *Lonicera × heckrottii* 'Gold Flame' (honeysuckle)

p. 130: *Penstemon* 'Blackbeard' (beardtongue)

p. 133: *Tulipa* 'White Triumphator'

p. 134-135: *Orlaya*

p. 137: Yarrow *Achillea millefolium*

p. 139: *Nepeta racemosa* 'Walker's Low' (catmint)

p. 141: Sweet alyssum

p. 142: *Lilium* 'Scheherazade'

p. 145: Common dandelion *Taraxacum officinale*

p. 146: Genovese basil *Ocimum basilicum*

p. 148-149: *Gaura* 'Whirling Butterflies'

p. 150: *Phlox paniculata* (garden phlox, unknown variety)

p. 153: Zinnia 'Oklahoma White', Cosmos 'Sensation Radiance', flowering tobacco *Nicotiana sylvestris*

p. 154: *Heuchera* 'Northern Exposure' (coral bells)

p. 156: top: dandelions and *Orlaya*; bottom: alpine strawberry 'Mignonette'

p. 158: *Rubus fruticosus* 'Chester' (thornless blackberry)

p. 160-161: *Rubus fruticosus* 'Chester' (thornless blackberry)

p. 163: American elderberry *Sambucus canadensis*

p. 164: *Paeonia lactiflora* 'Shirley Temple' (peony)

p. 166: *Phlox paniculata* 'Jeana'

p. 169: *Allium aflatunense* 'Purple Sensation' (purple allium)

p. 174: *Physalis pruinosa* 'Aunt Molly's' (ground cherry)

p. 176: *Cornus Florida* 'Cherokee Princess' (flowering dogwood tree)

p. 180: Snapdragon 'Chantilly Light Salmon'

p. 182: Clockwise from top left: *Galanthus* 'Sam Arnott' (snowdrop), *Tulipa* 'White Triumphator', dahlia (unknown variety), drumstick allium *Allium sphaerocephalon*

p. 184: Pothos

p. 189: Bird pepper

p. 190: Zigzag goldenrod *Solidago flexicaulis*

p. 196: Poppy 'Lauren's Grape'

ABOUT
THE AUTHOR

CHRISTIE PURIFOY is a writer and gardener who loves to grow flowers and community. She is the author of *Garden Maker: Growing a Life of Beauty and Wonder with Flowers; Roots and Sky: A Journey Home in Four Seasons;* and *Placemaker: Cultivating Places of Comfort, Beauty, and Peace.*

Christie earned a PhD in English literature from the University of Chicago but eventually traded the classroom for an old Pennsylvania farmhouse called Maplehurst, where, along with her husband and four children, she welcomes frequent guests to the Maplehurst Black Barn.

BLACK BARN
GARDEN CLUB

Whether you are an aspiring gardener or an experienced one, Christie would love to welcome you into the Black Barn Garden Club, an online membership community committed to cultivating wonder at blackbarngardenclub.com. You can also learn more about Christie at christiepurifoy.com, or connect with her and discover more about life at Maplehurst on Instagram @christiepurifoy and @maplehurstgardens.

With her longtime friend and fellow writer Lisa-Jo Baker, Christie hosts the *Out of the Ordinary* podcast where they help listeners grow a daily life that matters. New episodes are shared each Wednesday.

Together, Christie and Lisa-Jo and a community known as the Black Barn Collective turn social media's usual ways upside down through quiet, weekly rhythms of listening, sharing, and celebrating in a virtual gathering placed called the Black Barn Online. You are invited to join them at blackbarnonline.com and help tend a space where art and faith cultivated in a community take root, flourish, and grow.

MORE REFLECTIONS FROM CHRISTIE ON THE WONDERS OF GARDENING

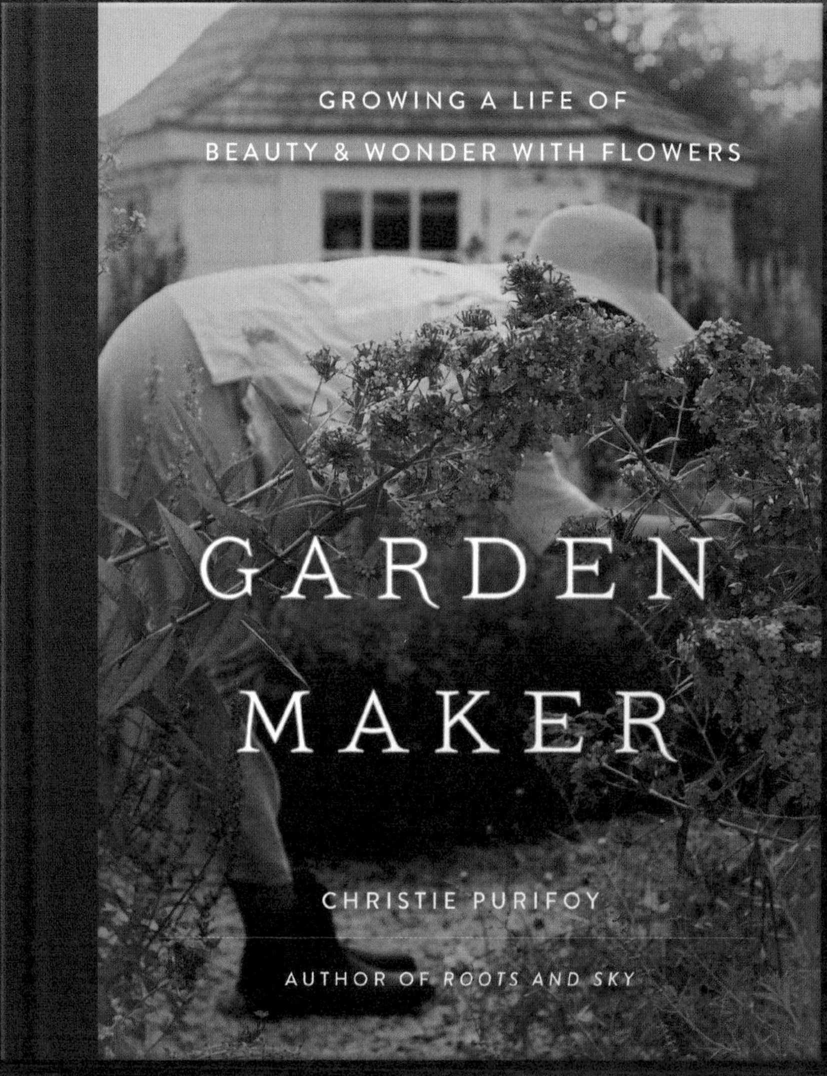

GROWING A LIFE OF
BEAUTY & WONDER WITH FLOWERS

GARDEN
MAKER

CHRISTIE PURIFOY

AUTHOR OF *ROOTS AND SKY*

Much more than a how-to flower gardening book, *Garden Maker* is
for those who want to grow beautiful things that reflect the glory and
majesty of the creator and bring a little bit of heaven down to earth.

FOUR ENCHANTED SEASONS

WITH FLOWERS

A HOME
in bloom

CHRISTIE PURIFOY

AUTHOR OF *GARDEN MAKER*

This beautifully photographed guide shows you how to enjoy the
many gifts the garden offers inside your own home, transforming
your living spaces into places filled with warmth and wonder.

Unless otherwise indicated, all Scripture quotations are taken from the Holy Bible, New International Version®, NIV®. Copyright © 1973, 1978, 1984, 2011 by Biblica, Inc.™ Used by permission of Zondervan. All rights reserved worldwide. www.zondervan.com. The "NIV" and "New International Version" are trademarks registered in the United States Patent and Trademark Office by Biblica, Inc.™

Verses marked ESV are taken from the ESV® Bible (The Holy Bible, English Standard Version®), copyright © 2001 by Crossway, a publishing ministry of Good News Publishers. Used by permission. All rights reserved.

Cover and interior design by Faceout Studio
Cover and interior graphics © Ekaterina Romanova / Getty Images; Some design elements © olga.korneeva / Creative Market; Image (woodgrain) pages 204 and 205 © Zocha_K / iStock

For bulk, special sales, or ministry purchases, please call 1-800-547-8979.
Email: Customerservice@hhpbooks.com

ℳ® This logo is a federally registered trademark of the Hawkins Children's LLC. Harvest House Publishers, Inc., is the exclusive licensee of this trademark.

SEEDTIME AND HARVEST

Text and photographs copyright © 2024 by Christie Purifoy
Published by Harvest House Publishers
Eugene, Oregon 97408
www.harvesthousepublishers.com

ISBN 978-0-7369-8218-4 (hardcover)
ISBN 978-0-7369-8219-1 (eBook)

Library of Congress Control Number: 2023936279

Printed in China

23 24 25 26 27 28 29 30 31 / RDS–FO / 10 9 8 7 6 5 4 3 2 1